GOD IS A POTATO

GOD IS A POTATO

The Wisdom of a Tibetan Monk

CHRISTINA MALEA

For the Divine Source, the Infinite Intelligence,

for every co-creative soul I have met or will meet,

for Everything and Nothing,

my endless gratitude.

Namaste!

Contents

"Each of us is a God.
Each of us knows all.
We need only open our minds to hear our own wisdom."

— Buddha

Introduction

God is a Potato! For those who await the "Final Judgment," such an utterance could be blasphemous. But, let me assure you, God has a sense of humor. Within a few hours of mulling whether to name a book *"God is a Potato,"* I was asking for a sign that would help decide if this book was indeed a good idea — essentially saying: *"Ok, Big Boss of the Universe, if writing this book is a good idea, I need a sign."* A few hours later, I stumbled upon a potato on the sidewalk. You might think that these events — the spontaneous idea of writing a book whose content and title you can literally see in front of your eyes, and then a few hours later stumbling upon a potato on the sidewalk — is a coincidence, a miracle, a divine sign, or something amusing. In my case, it is also a fact. And an extraordinary one at that, when on an ordinary, clean street where there's no market or dumpster that would explain why a potato is lying on the road, there it was. I think that if I had ignored this sign, the next one would have been to bump my head against the stop sign at the crossroads. At the time, I could practically hear my spiritual guide saying that if I ignored this occurrence, the next sign would be a potato hitting my head. The truth is that, in the end, this incident made me reflect on the fact that God, the Divine Energy, or whatever you want to call Him, often speaks to us in unusual, even amusing ways. We don't always pay attention to these signs, either because we miss them entirely, fail to reach beyond our senses, or because we simply consider signs to be "random happenings."

But before I go any deeper into the heart of this story, let me tell you a bit about the context of this book, which is *my* story. Born and raised in a Christian family, I lived the first years of my childhood in an environment where religion was present but not fanatical. At least that's how I perceived it at the time. My family was Christian, but I never felt the rigid and fanatical pressure that some people have felt. I fondly remember those childhood years when I spent summer holidays in the countryside. Lying between hills and mountains, the village where we stayed seemed magical to me. On Sundays, my grandmother would dress me and my brother in "good clothes" to go to the monastery for the sermon. My brother and I didn't feel forced to do it; rather, I liked going there. We rarely stayed for the whole sermon. Instead, we would go outside and play in the yard of the monastery. It seemed like a place out of a fairytale: surrounded by the hills wooded in green oaks; immersed in the warm summer morning sun; the scent of linden trees flooding everything around us; and colorful flowers as far as the eye could see. That place felt like heaven on earth. The village with its traditional houses could be seen from a distance, bees were humming busily from flower to flower, and we just breathed life. We didn't keep track of time. We didn't know if it was Tuesday or Wednesday. We didn't think of such things as years, days, or hours. We lived in a continuous present. My grandmother never forced us to do anything against our will, except to take a nap in the afternoon. It's funny how we hated afternoon naps then as much as we love them now, as adults. And while my grandmother taught us all kinds of prayers, and we went to the monastery every Sunday, this is not how I learned to be a good Christian. I didn't even know the concept of what it meant to be a "Christian" at that tender age. I simply learned what it meant "to be." I learned about kindness, gentleness and compassion from my grandmother's actions. And, when she died, I knew I would see her again. At the time I didn't understand what death meant, and I didn't know how I would see her again, but somehow I knew our reunion would come to be eventually.

Despite this knowing, my relationship with God was not the best after my grandmother passed away, in large part because the years following were a nightmare. I nearly hated Him because I was born in a country that defines injustice, corruption at all levels. It was also the period when everything around me seemed to collapse. I knew that God punishes bad people, but my inner child didn't understand what I had done so wrong to deserve so much pain. Later, school and society left me with beliefs that stuck with me and defined the following years of my life — *"we have only one life," "fear God," "the poor go to heaven and the rich go to hell,"* and many others. They probably sound familiar to you. My subconscious had assimilated these beliefs, but I felt inside that there was something wrong with them even if I couldn't exactly define what it was.

It wasn't until a few years of depression, when I lived and endlessly rolled over in my mind a past that was long over, that I came across a book that was to be the trigger for me getting out of that situation. That's how I came to know the power of a book and why I am deeply grateful for each page I've laid my eyes on. This book presented me with two options: either to endlessly iterate that pain, or to change my life. Realizing that the second option was available to me and that I could change my life. At first, I set out on an old-fashioned path to change, with the carrot dangling in front of the donkey. You know — a career, climbing the corporate ladder, money, a house, a family. There's nothing wrong with having these things. And for me, it seemed to be a promising path to the change at that moment. So, I set off with enthusiasm, just like a real little donkey to reach my carrots, believing that this was the way I would feel an authentic happiness of being. But at some point, something happened that would change the rest of my life. A whispered voice told me that no matter what I had or obtained in this life, I wouldn't be truly happy until I found *"something."* Of course, at first, I ignored that voice because the carrots in front of the donkey looked very good. Besides, I thought that maybe I had eaten something bad and was hallucinating, which was another reason to ignore it. I kept ignoring that experience until it showed up again. This time, however, the experience was much more intense. Not only was I told the same thing again, but it was much more real to me. I sensed that I had absolutely everything I desired right in front of my eyes — the perfect relationship, the perfect house, and the key of my dream car in my hand — but all I could feel was an immense inner void and such a miserable unhappiness that it seemed to swallow me. At that moment, my "success" had turned into the greatest failure of my existence. And, since that moment, my life has been like a roller coaster in search of that *"something."*

I've looked for *it* in all kinds of religions, and everywhere outside myself, until I decided to search the one place I hadn't looked: inside myself. Finally, then after years of searching, I came to understand and feel what that *"something"* is and means. It's not something material, it's not something you can buy, it's not something you can lose and it's not something you can define. It is what *YOU* truly are, beyond any cover, beyond any ideology, nationality, or religion. Discovering and living according to this *True Self* is the sublime experience you can live in this life. In the end, this is one of the purposes of life, to come here and discover who you are through what you are not, to brush off the dust and discover that you are love through every ounce of your person, to discover that you are a perfect Divine Being in your imperfection, and finally to reach the wisdom of understanding that God is a Potato!

Chapter 1

The Steep Trails of Tibet

MONK: So, dear soul, what brings you to the heart of the East?

WOMAN: ...

MONK: It's hard to believe you came all this way only to see an old Tibetan man at the end of the world. I know the journey here wasn't easy, and few have the courage to cross the steep trails of this place for a mere autograph.

WOMAN: I didn't know that enlightened masters could be funny too.

MONK: They can choose to be anything, whatever they want. We can all choose who we want to be. Everything else is just preconceptions about "what someone or something should be like." These are just images created by people about other people. Do you think God is an old man who sits on a cloud and hands out punishments if you don't go to church, confess, or fast? That's just an image you've created about Him.

WOMAN: Maybe ... nothing is as it seems anymore.

MONK: That's because nothing is as it seems. I can hear the helplessness in your voice. So, what brings you to the end of the world?

WOMAN: Some time ago, I had a strange experience that has made a big impact on my last few years. I don't know how to explain it ....

MONK: We can start from the beginning. Let your emotions choose your words. We have all the time in the world.

WOMAN: Well, I've always believed that happiness means those things people fight for all their lives — the perfect relationship, a family, a house, a car. But at some point, when I was ready to choose that path, something happened. I don't know if it was a feeling or an inner voice, but a few years ago, I felt that no matter what I achieved in life, I would never be truly happy until I discovered "something." At that moment, I ignored that whispering voice, but after a while it came back and it was much more intense ... much more real. It was as if I had the key to my dream car, the perfect house, relationship, and family in my hand at that moment, but I felt absolutely and totally unhappy. In fact, "unhappy" is an understatement. I felt a cold shiver down my spine and the most tremendous inner void, the greatest misery, suffering and soul pain I had ever felt. At that point, I fell to my knees and started crying until I felt my eyes dried out and no more tears ran down my cheeks. It was as if my success had become empty and meaningless, as if that success turned out to be the greatest failure.

MONK: Hmm ... it seems you chose to wake up. This is indeed wonderful! We can celebrate.

WOMAN: Is it wonderful? Did I make this choice? To wake up?

MONK: It was your choice! We could say that your soul made this choice, but your soul only shows you several directions for you to choose from. In the end, you have the free will to choose, so this shouldn't surprise you. Every moment, you recreate yourself through the decisions you make and the experiences you live. However, you can say that the soul chooses the places and the people. You don't think we've met here by chance, do you? Nothing is fortuitous, and this is not just a mere cliché we hear more and more often. There is order in chaos. There is peace in violence. There is love in hate. There is silence in noise, just as there is noise in silence.

WOMAN: Okay, my soul showed me several options, I chose, but I don't understand why everything had to be so vague. Why wasn't I told from the beginning exactly what I needed to find out? What am I supposed to understand by that discovery of a "something" missing?

MONK: Do you think you would have had the level of awareness necessary to understand what you needed to find out if that "something" had been revealed to you all at once and at that moment? What do you think happens to someone who has only been in darkness, and suddenly a strong light shines in front of their eyes? They become blind! Do you think you would have understood the Intelligence of the Universe if it had been suddenly revealed to you?

WOMAN: Probably not. I would probably have felt overwhelmed by all the information. I don't think I could have learned so many things.

MONK: It's not about learning. You said it yourself, from your own experience. You weren't told to "learn something." You were told to *"find something,"* which implies that you already know it. Life is a journey of remembering, not a journey of learning. You have nothing to learn here, only to remember who and what you truly are! You already know everything. Earth is not a school where you learn something. It is the place where you remember what you truly are, and finding out and feeling what you truly are, beyond nationality, religion, politics or any ideology, is one of the greatest achievements in this life. At the center of your being, you already have the answer.

You know who you are and you know what you want.

WOMAN: So, is it true? That so-called "amnesia" before coming here? Do we simply forget everything?

MONK: Of course! Hasn't the West normalized this yet? How do you think you can recreate yourself again and again? You recreate yourself with every experience you convey by living through the *True You*.

WOMAN: The True Me?

MONK: Let's start from the fact that there is no "*good-evil,*" "*love-hate,*" "*beautiful-ugly,*" and so on. These labels exist only in the relative world we live in, since at a spiritual level, you are love, just love. You are love, which is a concept. Are you following me? You don't know what love means as an experience because you need an experience that involves polarity in order to define and understand it. So, you experience hate or other complementary feelings in order to come to an understanding of love. It's the same with light or any other concept: you wouldn't understand what light means without darkness, right? Darkness is not against us. It tries to shape us. When we understand this, we can use darkness as a tool to obtain light. That's why you can't judge polarity. You can't judge matter. These are part of the third dimension we belong to. You need to understand the purpose of transformation. The good part is when you realize that you are stuck in the world of matter. Why? Because this is when you start to consciously transform your reality into another. The unpleasant part, if we can say so, is when you are stuck in the reality of matter but you say no to transformation, no to change. When you refuse change, the entire vibration of your body and reality starts to change you by force, because the main purpose of the Universe is evolution. If you don't change, the energy is blocked, and blocking energy means illness, war, cataclysms, or any other calamity. Energy is the greatest source of power. It is the currency of the Universe.

Money is not the ultimate currency, but energy is. When you are in a high vibration of love and gratitude, you will receive the same energy reflected back to you. That's why they say that "*you reap what you sow,*" because this is indeed true. Thus, illness or war is just your final product, when you don't realize that you need to change. Therefore, the Universe will force you to change. Ultimately, we need to understand that if we want to get rid of illness, war, and other disasters, we must not fight against them. You can't use peace to fight war, you can't use health to fight illness because they are part of the polarity of the dimension we are in. When you fight illness, all the efforts to create healing practically do nothing but strengthen the reality of the illness. You can't fight a dimension, but you can transcend it. This is when polarity disappears. However, in this dimension, war and peace mean polarity. There will always be a need for peace and war if you are in polarity. But if you use peace to fight war, then peace becomes war.

WOMAN: These are just sophisms! Utter nonsense! Nothing makes sense! How can peace become war?

MONK: Just imagine you are in the middle of a large room. One side of the room is lit by a candle, while the other side is in complete darkness. Now, move towards the light! What do you think will happen? Your shadow will become larger and larger until it engulfs the light of the candle. Light becomes darkness. That's why, when you ascend to a higher dimension, such as the fifth dimension, you will realize that war and peace exist as reality because we cannot or do not want to evolve alone. Thus, peace and war begin to disappear when you are in harmony, in tune with the change in your own life. This is when you find the middle way — balance and harmony.

WOMAN: Are you saying that the fifth dimension is like seeing in front of your eyes the film you are the director of? As if I were looking at Earth from somewhere above and I knew that everything that is happening has a purpose?

MONK: Precisely!

WOMAN: What exactly are these dimensions? Since there is a fifth dimension, it means there are several dimensions.

MONK: Of course, these dimensions are different modes of consciousness in which you observe reality. One is not superior to another. They are not linear. For example, the sixth dimension was born from the third dimension, and the third from the sixth. What we need to know is that the only way to go through each dimension is through the heart, not the mind. The heart is the only one that can feel before understanding. The dimensions are nothing but different perspectives of the same truth. Imagine that the truth is a sphere. You can't see all the perspectives at the same time. Our only purpose is to know ourselves through as many dimensions as possible and thus live the truth from each dimension and perspective. The first dimension is unity, it is mentality, it is thought. Unity is the only place we come from and the only place we go to. The second dimension is duality. It appeared as a response to experimentation. Imagine a person who has read thousands of books but hasn't experienced any. This is the first dimension. Then, the need to experience things appeared, and the second dimension was born, where you experience the scenario of a book. The second dimension is built on two perspectives: positive and negative. Negative, in this case, is not synonymous with "*bad.*" It means that the state of neutrality needs both perspectives — positive and negative — to exist, just like Yin and Yang. The third dimension consists of spirit, soul and body ... or vibration, energy, and matter. The third dimension, the one we are in, allows us to see and experience the second dimension, the positive and the negative, from a single place. That's why we have the third eye, which is located in the sixth chakra. We have two eyes, a positive one and a negative one, as well as a third eye located between the other two, through which we can see both perspectives from a single angle. The fourth dimension is the one that shapes time, in order for you to see and explore the possibilities of every decision you have made in life, every step you have taken, every consequence. You can see the past, the present and the future at the same time. While the third dimension is the expression of space, we can say that the fourth dimension is the expression of time. The fifth dimension is that eye that sees everything from above and understands the whole process. It is the dimension where the wise, those who have completed the third dimension, can look at the expression, at the whole process of the fourth dimension and understand why, what the purpose is.

WOMAN: Can you refer to a concrete example?

MONK: Of course! War is seen as something negative, or bad, in our dimension, right?

WOMAN: Yes, but war is something bad in any dimension.

MONK: Not really. You see, in the fifth dimension, it is not something negative. If the planet doesn't evolve willingly or evolves very, very slowly, because we are caught in the illusion of the material world, then wars, diseases, pandemics, crises, and natural disasters are triggers for change. Have you noticed that after every so-called "world catastrophe," the greatest leaps in evolution have occurred? That's why, in the fifth dimension, we have masters or spiritual guides who guide us to our purposes in life, whispering to us what is good, what is bad, what to do, or what not to do. They see the whole picture. The fifth dimension is connected to the third one, since it helps us understand the process, why we live in the third and fourth dimensions. That's why the guides from the fifth dimension help us in the third dimension. It's a perfect symbiosis. We help them feel and experience, and they help us by guiding us, because they are above our experience and can see the whole picture. Is it clearer now?

WOMAN: Yes, thank you! We can move on.

Chapter 2

A Cake Soaked in Syrup

MONK: Good, then let's review the first five dimensions because we have four more to cover. Everything began with the first dimension, and then reality started to split into two, creating the second dimension which includes the positive and the negative. We experience the second dimension, with the positive and the negative, in the third dimension through matter. The fourth dimension gives us the context of time to experience every space and time frame. The fifth dimension helps us see the purpose, the *"why,"* of this experience. Moving forward to the sixth dimension, we find a realm where our understanding of good and evil dissolves. Here is where we find architects of reality who know how to build entire universes, as they are free from the limits of time and space. The sixth dimension, without the bounds of time and space, is the place where you create your own realities. The seventh dimension is the dimension of perfect harmony, the dimension of heaven. Here, we encounter the seven laws of the Universe. In this dimension, there is no longer the need to create anything, there is only the happiness of experience. The eighth dimension is where we have access to the Akashic records. Here, we can contemplate every possible expression of what the mind of the Universe creates.

WOMAN: This dimension seems quite vague.

MONK: We can think of it as the great tree of life, where the roots meet the branches like in a network of connections linking everything that exists within a collective consciousness. You can look at it this way. And lastly, there is the ninth dimension. Well, the ninth dimension is the dimension of God. It is a place where there is no light, only void. The ninth dimension is like a black hole. It is the place from where we understand how the Universe sees itself. Here, time and space end, there is no coherence of the states of being. Here, you no longer feel anything. We won't go into more details about what each dimension means because this is an endless discussion. It's enough to know roughly what each one means and to know that being in the third dimension doesn't mean you can't reach other dimensions here. As I said before, it's important to remember that the only way to pass through each dimension is through the heart, not through the mind. Knowing each dimension is essential because this is the only way to return to yourself. This is how you will understand the perfection of creation.

WOMAN: But how can I experience these dimensions here?

MONK: Through awareness, through change, through evolution ... by living according to your *True You*, your *True Self*.

WOMAN: You keep repeating this idea of the "*True Self*" and I don't understand. Am I not my *True Self*? I know who I am, I know my name, my age, I know where I came from and what I've been through.

MONK: What is a name?

WOMAN: I don't understand the question. It's obvious. Since the very beginning, each person has a name. Our parents generally choose the name.

MONK: So, we both agree that your name is just a label given by your parents. Your age is just a number that identifies every year in a relative temporal Universe. We say my name, my age, my hands, my feet, my body…. We say my thoughts, my emotions, right? They are not me. They are mine. I am not my thoughts and emotions. Then … who am I? Who am I to whom all these temporary identities belong?

WOMAN: I've never thought about this perspective! We are so deeply grounded in our world that we easily identify with both our thoughts and our emotions. Moreover, we even define ourselves through the possessions we have, thinking we are this or that if we own certain things.

MONK: Exactly! And as long as you act and define your own experience according to the theology of a religion, the philosophy of a certain policy, or "the right way to do things," you are not acting according to your *True Self*. What's even sadder, is that most people live and act according to the truth of others, which they adopt as their own truth.

WOMAN: I don't understand. Can you expand on that?

MONK: Not acting according to your own truth is more painful than death itself. In fact, death isn't even painful, but we will talk about this and its meaning later. So, not acting according to your own truth is like denying your own self. You are the only one responsible for both your happiness and your unhappiness. Your parents or your family are, in turn, responsible for their own happiness. You didn't come into the world to meet someone else's expectations. Taking responsibility can be a foreign concept to those who leave decisions to fate or to anyone or anything other than themselves. How often have you done something just because someone else said that "you had to" or "that was the right way to do it"? Even when you think that "life is hard," a thought people reference so often, you are not living according to your own truth.

WOMAN: But life is hard! There's so much filth, famine ... there are so many wars, crimes and natural disasters all over the world ...

MONK: Is it?

WOMAN: Maybe because you live here isolated, hidden from the world in the heart of the mountains, you don't know what's happening out there.

MONK: Don't I? Do you know why masters are never affected by such "disasters"?

WOMAN: Because they are isolated in the heart of the mountains and don't care about what's happening in the world?

MONK: Because they see polarity from the fifth dimension. Because they have reached a level where not only do they know that there is no such thing as "*God-Satan*," "*good-evil*," "*health-illness*," "*war-peace*," or "*heaven-hell*," but they also *feel* this truth and they live it. This knowledge is part of them, part of every cell in their bodies. Knowing is not enough; you have to live, integrate, and embody these things as part of yourself. Knowing that love is good doesn't help you if you don't absorb this truth and act in accordance with it. Imagine a cake that needs to be soaked in syrup. You are the cake, and the syrup is love or gratitude. When the cake is soaked, every part of it absorbs the sweet syrup. This is exactly the kind of love, gratitude and faith we are talking about, in which every atom of your body vibrates with these emotions. Do you think I have always been a Buddhist monk? I was an engineer.

WOMAN: I can't believe it! There's no connection between spirituality and engineering or science in general.

MONK: There will be one when you want to make a connection. All roads lead to the same place, regardless of what life looks like. Our daily routine can't be separated from our spiritual evolution because this is actually our spiritual life! May I continue and tell you about my experience? When I was little, I hated Math and Physics, but my father wanted me to become an engineer, and after years of study, I became an engineer. I considered those years the worst of my life, as I was bound by the rigidity of calculations and theories. Then, a few years after dedicating my life to a purpose my soul had been longing for and becoming a monk, I realized that all those years I had considered "the worst of my life" proved to be some of the best years of my life. I understood how much science and spirituality are connected and how much those years helped me understand this. The Universe, through its spiritual dimensions, is geometry. The octahedron, tetrahedron, and other geometric shapes are spatial representations of the dimensions we've just talked about. The Fibonacci sequence from mathematics is also found in nature, in seeds, fruits, and vegetables. So, nothing is separate in this world, no matter how much it may seem that there's no connection. In the end, disease, famine, wars or any personal crisis, anything "*bad*" ... all these things are neither good nor bad. They are part of the polarity, part of the experience of souls, and represent their evolution. Wars, pandemics, all crises make us detach from the material world and send us inside ourselves.

WOMAN: Do we really have to go through so much pain for evolution?

MONK: We don't have to do anything. These things happen because we allow them to happen, because, as I said before, we resist change and evolution, and the Universe forces us through other means to evolve. Ultimately, we don't truly realize the impact of our thoughts, which travel through the Universe and return to us exactly like a boomerang. Nothing that exists is as it is by nature. If it were, then that neighbor at the end of the street would be perceived the same by everybody, either obnoxious or kind, but this isn't the case. For his family, he may be the best person in the world, while to the neighbor across the street he may be a cocky braggart he cannot stand. Or a kitchen knife would be seen by everyone either as a good object or as a bad one. But this doesn't happen because someone who cuts bread with it to make a delicious sandwich considers it an indispensable utensil, while someone else may see it as a diabolical item because it represents a murder weapon. So, you see, no one and nothing is as it is by nature. Everything has a state of neutrality, of balance, of void, of absolute zero.

WOMAN: Then what makes an object or an action good or bad?

MONK: You! The way you see things is the result of patterns you've imprinted over time, when you did, said or thought something good or bad about a person or interacted with an object in similar situations of thinking or acting. A dog is neither good nor bad. It's simply in a neutral state, possessing the characteristics of hidden potential. For some people it can be a bad animal because, in their childhood, they were bitten by a dog. For other people, it can be the most adorable animal in the world, and they can show you countless pictures capturing its beauty and cuteness. So, your mind is what labels things, the energy with which you cover everything around you.

WOMAN: Incredible! I can't believe it! That's an interesting way of seeing things.

MONK: I'm glad we agree. So, I think we can sum it all up in one word — energy.

WOMAN: Informally, we call it a "vibe." Science calls it energy. Religion calls it spirit. But I think they all refer to the same thing, don't they?

MONK: That's right! Your observation is very good. So, this energy flows through us, through our chakras, just as electrical energy flows through cables and wires. Opening the chakras is an intense experience. The first chakra is Muladhara or the root chakra, located at the base of the spine. It's responsible for survival and courage and it's blocked by fear. The next chakra is called Svadhisthana or the sacral chakra and it's responsible for pleasure and passion. It's blocked by guilt. The third chakra or Manipura is located in the stomach area. This chakra governs willpower and it's blocked by shame. The fourth chakra or Anahata is situated in the heart area. It governs love and it's blocked by grief and suffering. Vishuddha or the fifth chakra is positioned in the throat area. It governs the truth and it's blocked by the lies we tell ourselves and by not expressing our *True Self*. The sixth chakra is Ajna, the light chakra, located in the center of the forehead. It governs intuition and understanding, seeing beyond the senses, which is also why it's called the third eye. We have two eyes to perceive the physical world and a third eye to understand things beyond our senses. This third eye is blocked by illusion. The seventh chakra, Sahasrara or the crown chakra, is situated on top of the head. It's responsible for spirituality, cosmic energy, and it's blocked by ego, earthly attachments. These are the seven main chakras most of us know. Of course, apart from them, we also have secondary chakras, but for now, it's enough for you to know these ones.

WOMAN: So, is the seventh chakra the most important?

MONK: No one chakra is more important than the others. You see, each chakra is represented by a law of the Universe. The seventh chakra is the chakra of mentalism. Are you the result of your ideas? Are you what you think? The sixth chakra is the chakra of correspondence. What is inside you is reflected on the outside, like a mirror. Ask yourself if what you feel inside corresponds to what you see outside. The fifth chakra is the chakra of vibration. Ask yourself if you are expressing your own truth or hiding it in silence. The fourth chakra is the chakra of rhythm. Do you respect the time of evolution, the time of your life? Do you understand its rhythm? Are you in coherence with it? The third chakra is the chakra of cause and effect. Look around and ask yourself what is happening in your life, as you are the cause affecting your own life. The second chakra is the chakra of polarity. Ask yourself if you fight against polarity or understand that it helps us evolve and is not a reason for separation. The first chakra is the chakra of creation. We are creators in these bodies. Emotionally, mentally, and physically we are made to create, not to destroy. The goal is the coherence of all chakras. All of them are equally important and, to live in balance and in harmony, all of them must communicate. These chakras are like lakes connected to one another. Imagine seven lakes stretching one behind the other and being connected by small channels. They communicate with each other, linked together like a chain. What do you think happens in nature if a lake no longer communicates with its water source?

WOMAN: I suppose it turns into a swampy puddle when it becomes stagnant.

MONK: The exact same process happens in the human body. Those energy spheres that no longer flow start to create blockages that, sooner or later, can trigger the appearance of physical diseases. Thus, we end up resorting to all sorts of medications that only treat the symptoms and not the root cause. In the end, we enter a vicious circle, from which only awareness can save us. So, it all comes down to energy, dear soul! I don't think we need to further develop this topic. Your Western science has already explored this field through quantum physics, metaphysics, and other disciplines. There are countless books that reiterate the fact that everything is energy, including the wooden table or the tea cup in front of you. The way we act in each situation represents an imprinted energy. Our thoughts and feelings are energy. With them, every day, we create a reality of either health and peace or illness and conflicts.

WOMAN: That sounds kind of harsh. It doesn't feel like we have that kind of power.

MONK: We actually do, and we use it every second, every day, consciously or unconsciously, influencing the reality around us. Not to mention collective thoughts and emotions, which are truly sublime. Some time ago, I joined several monks and ordinary people from Tibet and around the world, to meditate together simultaneously, each in their own part of the world. The purpose of the meditation was to stop an imminent war that was about to start between two nations in the Middle East. Our meditation, thoughts, and feelings channeled peace, love, and harmony in that direction. What do you think happened? A peace agreement was signed between the two nations, which would have seemed impossible at a first glance. Apparently, it was a *"miracle,"* but this was merely something normal, like bringing rain to the desert, healing the most terrible diseases, and so on. You see, when we experience what seems impossible, we often label the event as a miracle, but once it has happened, this event opens a door to even more possibilities. In one word, everything is energy, dear soul. As soon as you realize the greatness of this truth, a world full of *"miracles"* will unfold before you, which are nothing else but our divine nature. That's why imagining God as an old man with a beard sitting on a cloud throwing down punishments is pure madness. He is God, He is Buddha, He is Jesus, He is the Divine Intelligence, He is You! He is Everything and Nothing. The Alpha and the Omega. He is good and evil, beautiful and ugly, woman and man, health and illness, He is in the raindrops that trickle down the window, the sea breeze that touches your skin, the scratches and bruises you used to get as a child when you played and fell, He is the tea in your teacup.

WOMAN: Is He a Potato?

MONK: God is a Potato!

WOMAN: That would sound like blasphemy to most people. Even in this century, you'd probably be burned at the stake for uttering such a thing.

MONK: As I said — God is a Potato! If you looked through a microscope at a tiny piece of a potato, you'd see a whole Universe there. Then you'd understand why God is a Potato. Everything is created from the same matter, only that in different forms, like the fingers of a hand. Each finger has its own particularity, but all fingers are part of the same hand. The air in the living room might be different from the air in the kitchen where dinner is being prepared, but it's the same air. That's why *"you reap what you sow."* A punch in someone's face will ricochet back sooner or later to your own face because you're basically hitting yourself. We are one. We are separate and at the same time, we are one. If you understand this, you will understand that God is a Potato, that everything is created from the same matter in different forms and that there's no separation, only unity. God created us to express Himself through us in all possible forms and nuances. He expresses Himself through absolutely everything that exists: from beings to objects, stars, planets and galaxies. That's why believing He is vengeful when you fail to listen to Him is madness. How could He punish you or be vengeful when He gave you the free will to express yourself? Why would He have given you free will? He could have simply done things the way He wanted from the beginning. So, I will say it again — God is a Potato! God is instant soup! Do you have the courage to live this truth? Or is it *"inappropriate"* or *"a sin"*? Are you living your life according to your *True Self*? Because as a great master said, if you don't find out who you are, you will depend on the opinion of others who don't know who they are.

Chapter 3

You Need Faith

WOMAN: So, this is what you mean by your own truth, the *True Self*? When I fast, when I confess ... am I not living according to my own truth, but according to the truth of others who have defined these things as being "right"? Because sometimes I have the urge to enter a church but I don't do it because "I shouldn't" if I don't meet certain criteria. So, I'm not living according to my *True Self*, but according to the truth of others, and living according to the truth of others means I'm living the same experiences over and over again, instead of creating myself according to my own truth. Thus, I'm practically annihilating my own Who I Am, my *True Self*!

MONK: That's indeed blasphemy. And you do it every day, and then you wonder why you feel so miserable and blame the government, your family, anyone else, instead of taking responsibility for your own truth, the truth of your soul, and living it. You cannot simply blindly trust the ideas you grew up with, no matter who passed them on to you — your teachers, your parents, or the people around you. You cannot simply accept an idea, style, or other thing as being "right."

Pass them through the filter of your own thinking and through the filter of your own soul.

WOMAN: Easier said than done.

MONK: If this seems hard to you, then try translating a Tibetan book about the themes of human existence, the Buddhist sutras, or Buddha's early writings. It's hard to do it because you haven't managed to stop the background voices around you so you can listen to your own soul. Meditation, introspection, metacognition are just a few of the solutions that help you pay attention to your own thoughts. Do you think there's no reason for the dreams in your soul? Every day, people who truly want to sing, write, or become singers repress their desires because "life is hard," "you'll never make a living," "you have to be very talented," "you have to have connections," and all sorts of excuses. What happens then is that the soul, the inner child, begins to shout and cry because you don't listen to it. A warning, an accident, even a serious illness appears if small things like fatigue of any kind or sadness aren't listened to. That's how the death of the soul, that inner void that no one and nothing can fill, that death which is much more painful than physical death, begins. You know you're breathing, but are you really living?

WOMAN: It's really incredible! I've never thought that not living according to my own truth could have such consequences.

MONK: Indeed! Let me tell you about another blasphemy. The greatest criminals of history have reached Valhalla, Svarga, Heaven, or whatever you want to call it. Leaving aside the fact that they got there because there is no hell, a cauldron of boiling tar, they got there because they acted according to their own truth. Through their crusades, through all the crimes committed throughout history, they truly believed they were acting for the benefit of their country, nation, community.... So, they lived according to their *True Self*.

WOMAN: But this is total madness!

MONK: Is it really?

WOMAN: Of course it is!

MONK: If we think that those souls came to experience certain emotions, is this still madness? If Hitler's holocaust helped some souls figure out what forgiveness meant, and other souls discover their *True Self*, then is this still pure madness?

WOMAN: Not really, but the idea that we have to experience such suffering to evolve seems hard to accept.

MONK: The soul doesn't know what pain is. It just wants to grow and to experience as much as possible, and it's not anyone else's job to judge how it decides to do it.

WOMAN: These are just theories! Both the soul and the body know what pain is. The soul knows what pain is when it is betrayed by a loved one, while the body knows what pain is when it is hit.

MONK: That's because you chose for things to happen this way! But what would you say if you had chosen a different perception? Perception is something interesting. When we see the leaves of the trees moving, we think it's windy outside, but it could be a spirit wishing to make its presence felt. Of course, the only explanation for us is the wind because it's the only possible explanation from our point of view, or rather, from the database of limited perceptions we've gathered. So, what would you say if we altered perception and, instead of feeling pain when the person you love betrayed you, you felt gratitude for the lesson that came into your life ... maybe a lesson of trust and self-love, maybe a lesson of detachment, or perhaps a lesson of forgiveness. Perception creates reality. The same applies to the body. How do you think some people can walk on hot coal or jump into freezing water without showing a sign of suffering?

WOMAN: They are exceptions, just special people with special powers.

MONK: We are all special! It's just that some of us don't know it yet and wander in darkness, which is neither good nor bad, because to understand light, you must understand darkness. You shouldn't resist it, because anything you resist will persist; you should be the light in the darkness.

WOMAN: I don't understand. How can you do all this? Everything sounds so good and yet so hard to put into practice. I need your guidance.

MONK: No, you don't need my guidance. You need faith.

WOMAN: But I have faith!

MONK: We're not talking about rationalized faith, we're not talking about rationalized gratitude, we're not talking about rationalized love.... Such things cannot be rationalized. Remember the analogy with the cake soaked in syrup, or imagine a sponge thoroughly soaked in water. You can say the sponge is one with the water, that every cell in it is water. That's exactly the kind of faith I'm talking about, where every cell in your body is filled with faith, with gratitude, with love. This is because you already are all these things; you don't need to learn them, just remember them. To see, you must believe. Once, a great master said the following words: *"Faith means believing in the things we cannot see, and its reward is seeing the things we believe in."* Faith, as I said before, is not something that can be rationalized. It's simply the certainty through which the mind and the soul know that something is already fulfilled. This is also the secret of manifestation. Why do you think most people don't manifest in their lives what they desire? The secret of manifestation, which appears in most religions, is to believe that you already have that something. It's the energy of *knowing*, not the energy of *hoping*. I'm absolutely sure you've already had at least one such profound experience.

WOMAN: Now that I think about it, I believe I had such a moment of faith when I healed myself. A few years ago, I was in terrible pains, especially during the delicate days of the month. The solution was a surgery but, after the operation, I still had the same pains. Basically, every month I had that intense pain, which eventually led to fainting. I lived the following years with the same unbearable pain that made me faint. Despite dozens of medical tests and examinations from head to toe, no doctor could figure out what was wrong with me. At one point, I came across "*The Complete Dictionary of Ailments and Diseases,*" written by Jacques Martel, an extraordinary book that marked the beginning of my healing. This book helped me understand that all our health issues have emotional causes. Thus, I found out that my pains were caused by the rejection of femininity, as my energy was predominantly a masculine energy of "doing" rather than of "being." After a while, as if by miracle, this awareness and acceptance, along with the faith that I could be my old self before these pains, produced the healing, but not before I felt the most excruciating pains that made me unable to get out of bed. In those moments, perhaps even more than ever, I kept the same faith, the same image of myself completely healthy, and starting with the following month I no longer had such pains, nor fainting. I realized later that if I hadn't kept my faith during those critical moments of "test" pains, I probably would never have healed. Somehow, that crucial moment was exactly like the one when spaceships have to overcome gravity. Once they are past that critical moment of overcoming gravity, they can fly smoothly into space.

MONK: Beautiful experience and beautiful interpretation. I know Jacques Martel's book, a true divine inspiration of our times. Just as you said, most diseases have emotional triggers. Health means order, while disease means disorder. Organs, tissues and molecules are nothing but synchronized, ordered vibrations. When this energy or vibration desynchronizes, disease appears. We already know that emotions are energy in motion, and when they are blocked or there are certain deficiencies, they transform at a physical level into what we call diseases. Therefore, this awareness you had, along with your strong faith, even in spite of the seemingly contradictory events following your desire to get rid of those excruciating pains, ultimately led to healing. Related to this, Christians have an interesting passage in the Bible. When Jesus, besieged by an enthusiastic crowd, was going to heal the dying daughter of one of the synagogue leaders, a seriously ill woman touched his garments, hoping she would be cured that way. Then Jesus kindly says to her: "Daughter, your faith has healed you. Go in peace and be freed from your suffering." He said "*your faith,*" so he didn't take credit for her healing.

WOMAN: Indeed, it's exciting how things work themselves out in real life. I remember a few years ago, when one of my friends who had no health problems and was very active, suddenly collapsed and could no longer walk. All the tests he ran came out fine, and the doctors couldn't find any explanation for his condition. At that moment, he had to make an important decision regarding his business, which he kept postponing because he didn't know what to do next. What happened then was truly miraculous: after eventually making a final decision about his business, he could walk again.

MONK: All of life is a miracle, dear soul. Every day such healings considered "miracles" occur, but they are nothing but a natural state of being. As others have said before us, when you heal the inside, you automatically heal the outside. When your friend healed the inside, that is, when he made the decision that was holding him back and gnawing him inside, the healing on the outside also happened. After all, legs symbolize the relationship with advancement, with movement, with the power to move forward in life. When a health problem arises, my recommendation is that we should search inside and ask ourselves what was within us that triggered those problems, what emotions, what unsettled traumas led to those physical blockages. Jacques Martel's dictionary is an extraordinary tool that can be used in this regard, covering aspects from the most trivial health problems, like acne which is related to the management of emotions, to the most severe problems, like cancer.

WOMAN: After all, the problem of acne appears predominantly in teenagers, and it makes sense if we think about the fact that adolescence is like an emotional roller-coaster.

MONK: Exactly!

WOMAN: But how do we approach other problems apart from health issues? A dictionary for other problems would have been a good idea. Or at least a user's manual. Some consider the Bible to be such a manual.

MONK: It would probably have been an endless dictionary or user's manual, which ultimately wouldn't even be necessary, because you already have the answer to any problem inside you. Not in the Bible, but inside you. It's often like a whispered voice, while sometimes it's like intuition.

WOMAN: Do I already have the answer to any problem? I don't understand. Can you speak more plainly?

MONK: You think you are facing a problem when something or someone is bothering you, when an accident or illness occurs, right? Well, the answer is inside you, just like we said about health problems. When someone makes you feel in a way that creates frustration or discomfort, something inside you needs healing. Let's take an example. What bothers you right now?

WOMAN: Hmm ... when someone says something but doesn't keep their word. That drives me crazy. Just recently, one of my friends canceled a trip at the last minute for no real reason, even though she had promised me she would definitely come. I hate it when people don't keep their word. This time really drove me crazy and I'll admit I reacted impulsively.

MONK: Alright, now think of a situation, a moment from the past when you felt disappointed by something, by someone. Let's go back to your childhood. Usually, most patterns and traumas accumulate there. Basically, the adults of today are just the children of yesterday who carried their childhood traumas with them.

WOMAN: Now that you mention it, I do remember one experience in particular. When I was little, my parents promised they would let me go on school trips, but in the end, they never did. I never understood why. I would have probably preferred them to tell me from the beginning that they wouldn't let me go, instead of getting me to trust their words and then disappointing me. I really felt terribly disappointed, I felt my child-like trust be shattered.

MONK: Perfect, now we have the cause, or as I like to call it, the awareness. We have an unsettled event that has now come to light, meaning it has been acknowledged. Bring love and forgiveness to that situation, and you have created healing.

WOMAN: But how do I know I've healed?

MONK: Easy! When similar events happen again, and they surely will, they won't have the same impact on you, the same intensity. Eventually, they won't bother you at all. You will treat them with neutrality, perhaps even with joy. Try to be the observer of your own mind, and you will see this when someone promises something and doesn't keep their word next time, because healing or the lesson is always tested.

WOMAN: And what if it drives me crazy in the same way?

MONK: Then it means there are other similar situations to heal, but most of the time it's enough to reach just one of the causal memories for healing. In other words, most of the times, a single "Aha!" moment when discovering a similar situation is enough. So, the recipe is simple and within anyone's reach: recognize another similar situation, most often from childhood or from later on, then add love and forgiveness for that past situation, as well as for those you've attracted, because these situations only showed you that you have something to heal. You can apply a very simple technique for these situations — it's called Ho'oponopono and it consists of four sentences: "*I love you!*", "*I'm sorry!*" because I take responsibility for the entire existence, "*Forgive me!*", and "*Thank you!*". It's an extraordinary technique of a Hawaiian psychiatrist, Hew Len, who managed to heal an entire psychiatric ward of people with very serious mental issues by applying this method. Of course, this is just one of the techniques that can be applied. There are many others.

WOMAN: That's extraordinary! It means that in the same way, I can heal the wound of injustice, because I also detest unjust people. When I am treated unjustly, I become very impulsive and I react uncontrollably. When I was a child, I experienced situations of injustice when I felt wrongly accused of the mischief my sister did. I probably bottled-up feelings and emotions in those situations, and today I react accordingly.

MONK: Indeed! You see, you didn't say that thieves, murderers or leeches drive you crazy. You said that people who don't keep their word, unjust people bother you or drive you crazy because this was your wound to heal, the wound of injustice, the wound of betrayal.

WOMAN: It really makes sense.

Chapter 4

Honouring the Darkness

MONK: Imagine now what it would be like if you lived every moment with the same sublime awareness, with the same miraculous faith, and not just at certain sporadic moments. How would it be if you lived every moment in such a state of awareness, faith, gratitude, and love?

WOMAN: But it's so hard to keep this lifestyle at every second.

MONK: Is it? And yet you've managed to heal yourself. Isn't this exciting enough to make you choose it again and again? This is how the state of total awareness, of wisdom, the state of enlightenment is built. After all, the state of enlightenment can be reached by anyone; it's not something for the "chosen ones," and love is the path that leads us there.

WOMAN: Love ... what do you mean by love? I'm curious what love means to you. I'm sure almost all of us have experienced it at least once in our lives.

MONK: Love is eternity. It's not something you feel for others.

Love is the wave of time and space, it's not just the love for others. We make this mistake, and it's not surprising, considering that the Bible and sacred books in general talk about the love for others, but the interpretation of those words has been ambiguous. We believe that loving others is the only way to find balance, but it's not. Love is the main vibration that allows us to express ourselves. When you connect with the love of the Universe, you won't feel any emotion. You will feel every emotion in a single point because emotions are nothing but expressions of love. We can express love through different levels of vibration. For example, the opposite of love is not hate. Hate is just an expression with a low energy of love. You don't hate because you hate. You hate because you don't feel loved, right? You can understand every emotion through love, because love is the energy that creates every emotion.

WOMAN: What about unconditional love?

MONK: We often say that we love unconditionally, but we don't really know what it means. Unconditional means something that has no condition, right? You aren't capable of loving unconditionally if you have a condition. Even projection is a condition. What does projection mean? I am here, you are there. That's projection and implicitly it's a condition. You can't love the other if you don't realize that he or she is you from another perspective. Loving others means loving the perspective of yourself. The only way to love unconditionally is when you are coherent with yourself and love yourself. It's the only way. Love yourself in every possible projection of your own self.

WOMAN: I can't believe you've turned all my theories upside down. I don't think I've ever had so many "Aha!" moments. Now I understand why, the more I sacrifice for others thinking that this is love, the unhappier I feel.

MONK: Exactly, because constant sacrifice while neglecting your own needs leads to exhaustion and resentment. True unconditional love starts with self-love. When you love and respect yourself, you are able to offer yourself to others from a place defined by abundance, not by scarcity. As you have now realized, unconditional love doesn't mean sacrificing yourself, it means being in harmony with yourself and sharing that harmony with others. Unhappiness arises because you channel your love toward projections instead of focusing it on yourself. When you begin to genuinely and authentically love yourself, love will naturally project onto others without effort. The sunlight doesn't need to make an effort to reflect itself in the mirror. It simply reflects. The same happens with love. The Universe is the mirror. When you feel love for yourself, it will naturally reflect onto every being around you without any effort. We think we must fight for what is truly important, that such things require a tremendous effort. We even have these deeply ingrained preconceptions about love, thinking that complicated love is the most precious kind there is, and that we must fight for love. But you don't have to fight for love. If you have to fight, then it's not love. It is ego, obsession, attachment; it's anything you want, but not love.

WOMAN: If you have so much wisdom here, why don't you go out there and share it with everyone? Why do you keep it hidden? These words about what love truly means could be enough to change the lives of thousands, maybe millions, of people. We've been taught that love means sacrifice, that you have to fight for love, that love means loving others and forgetting about yourself. We've been taught that love means putting yourself last. So many people live with these preconceptions and misconceptions about love, thinking love is sacrifice and struggle. The West has gained the language of technology but has lost the language of wisdom, emotions, and prayer. Why do you keep all this wisdom hidden here?

MONK: But we aren't hiding anything. Truly important secrets are always hidden in plain sight. There are masters all over the world, but you don't listen to them or, if you do listen, things remain at a conceptual level without being put into practice. There are so many people who know theory so well but never apply anything. So, nothing changes.

WOMAN: Perhaps it's hard to get out of our comfort zones. I think we're like spaceships that need to overcome gravity to reach space. Overcoming gravity requires extraordinary power, but once you're in space, you don't need the same amount of energy. It's the same for us. The beginning is harder, so there needs to be discipline at first.

MONK: Beautiful analogy. Discipline that's another interesting word. Willpower and courage are its friends. Willpower is the force, the engine that allows wisdom and love to be expressed. It's the inner strength through which we understand that we are capable of anything. Never lose the courage to take risks, to explore new opportunities, or to be curious about your true nature. You are immortal, you cannot be hurt, you can never truly die. Love dissolves fear. Why should you be afraid? Fear paralyzes creation and intuition. We are infinite. You see, nothing is hidden. There are masters all over the world who talk about these things. We have even punished and crucified some of them.

WOMAN: You mean Jesus?

MONK: Jesus and many others. Buddha didn't come to boast that he had attained enlightenment. Jesus didn't come to boast that he could walk on water, heal, or turn water into wine. They came to show us what we can also do here on Earth. They didn't come to demand that churches and temples be built for them. They didn't come for us to worship them ... religion did all that. Spirituality and religion are totally different. They aren't the same thing. Religion is based on light and rejects darkness. Spirituality embraces darkness, because only through it can you get to know light. Religion has turned the voluntary love of God into the "fear of God." It has turned a loving God into a vengeful God who sends you to hell if you don't do things to His liking. Religion claims the superiority of man over woman. Why? Because long ago humanity separated men, who tried to reach the goal of light which was knowledge, from women, who worked at night in caves to achieve wisdom. Similarly, the patriarchal system created the idea that God was male. At some point, someone said that light was good so men were good, and since darkness was bad then every woman who worked at night in caves and forests to achieve wisdom had to be bad.

WOMAN: But aren't knowledge and wisdom the same thing? It sounds like men and women were fighting for the same thing.

MONK: Knowledge is not the same thing as wisdom. You aren't wise because you know things. You are wise because you understand things, because you feel them. Understanding is when you feel the truth. Long ago humanity split into good, which meant man, and bad, which meant woman. This happened because we disconnected from the Universe and connected only with the instinct of survival in this so-called "single life." You don't need to look too far to notice the consequences of these ideas even in this era of technology and evolution. Especially in the Arab world, not only there, but you can see how women are treated. So, when you understand duality, you will understand that every person you meet in life is nothing but a mirror of yourself. The people around you are simply mirrors. They reflect either something that is inside you, or something you judge, or something you have lost. For example, someone might appear in your life spontaneously and do something that makes you feel betrayed, revealing that you have an unhealed wound inside you. Another person might appear in your life and do something that makes you feel they didn't keep their word, revealing something you judge in others, because you look objectively from all angles and notice that you always keep your word, your promise. What is interesting is that, most of the time, these people who come into your life to teach you certain lessons will disappear as soon as you learn or remember those lessons ... because there's nothing to learn, only something to remember. No conscious effort is made to end these relationships. They will simply disappear because conversations will go from natural to forced and unnatural, maybe even meaningless. The Universe is just a mirror broken into many pieces. Each reflection you see in your life reveals something about you. Don't look at others with judgment, just observe what judgment lies within you. Then you can learn something new about yourself because of this duality.

WOMAN: Hmm ... interesting perspective! But what do you mean by that "something you have lost"? What kind of mirror is that?

MONK: Throughout life, we lose pieces of ourselves in various interactions with other people. Either they are taken from us by those who had power over us, or we lose them easily or give them to others with innocence and trust. That's why we sometimes feel obsessively attracted to certain people, because we see the missing pieces of ourselves in them; however, these pieces are never really missing, they are just forgotten or hidden deep within us over time. And it doesn't really matter what kind of mirror this is; the idea is that when something upsets or affects us, we should stop and think about what that reflection wants to tell us.

WOMAN: Why doesn't religion address more of these things?

MONK: Religion has caused more deaths than any epidemic or natural disaster. Haven't you ever wondered why religion, which preaches peace and love, has never managed to put into practice what it teaches? You've probably wondered because, if you had found the answers in religion, you wouldn't be here today. If you hadn't felt somewhere deep inside you that there was a different truth than the one preached by religions, or that these truths more or less contradict each other, your search would probably have already ended. And yet, every religion is what it is, and we shouldn't judge any of them.

Chapter 5

A CD Analogy: "Here" and "There"

WOMAN: It's true that no religion has truly answered my questions.

MONK: That's because they're incapable of answering all your questions. In divine writings, entire passages that have been altered and erased throughout history, so they certainly could not provide answers.

WOMAN: Altered writings? What do you mean by that?

MONK: Most Christians base their lives on the biblical scriptures without knowing that entire passages in the Bible have been changed or misinterpreted. In the past, when Christians became too numerous, Roman emperors found a way to control them from within through the holiest Christian writing — the Bible. The Romans altered certain passages to control the Christians much more easily. How could God be vengeful when He is the proclamation of love itself? How could He give you the most precious gift, namely the gift of free will, but at the same time punish you if you don't do something to His liking? What kind of free will is that?

WOMAN: I suppose a very confusing one.

MONK: The Bible also contained references to reincarnation, which were erased by the Roman Emperor Constantine the Great along with his mother Helena because they considered reincarnation a heresy. They believed that the power of the Church could thus be diminished and that people would have more time to seek salvation. However, references to reincarnation have always existed. Reincarnation had been included in the New Testament until the time of Emperor Constantine when the Romans censored it. Jesus himself believed in it when he asked the apostles if they had recognized Elijah reincarnated in John the Baptist. Elijah had lived nine hundred years before John. This is a fundamental doctrine of Jewish mysticism. Thus, with modified and erased passages, the religion of love became a religion of fear. Fear is the opposite of love. You see, the more we understand, the more we let go of fear and begin to truly live.

WOMAN: I understand. I don't know why, but for some reason I feel sad, disappointed by these things I've heard, but at the same time, I feel liberated.

MONK: I perfectly understand how you feel. It's normal to have mixed feelings when you discover or explore ideas that contradict what you have learned or been told. The feelings of sadness and disappointment come from the awareness of these disturbing aspects of history and misinterpretations. At the same time, liberation comes because you begin to see things from a broader and clearer perspective.

WOMAN: At least, since those masters who showed us the way were blamed and crucified, maybe we still have a chance with extra-terrestrial beings to save us. It seems that we don't learn much from humans.

MONK: Don't laugh! These beings are already doing that. These extraterrestrials, as you call them, these highly evolved beings, are already helping us. Do you think the fast evolution of technology and in consciousness in recent decades is a coincidence?

WOMAN: Hmm, probably not. But where are they hiding?

MONK: Do you think the only way to help someone is to show yourself in a form they recognize? How would that help? By repeating history? You would idolize them, build temples, and eventually it would all end with a New Age crucifixion. Help can come in multiple forms, through a spontaneous thought or a brilliant idea leading to a fantastic invention that can change people's lives.

WOMAN: So ... are you an extraterrestrial?

MONK: Maybe I am, maybe I'm not, maybe I am, maybe I'm not. I am what I am.

WOMAN: What a clear and straightforward answer ....

MONK: How would it help you if I either told you I was or wasn't an evolved being from another part of the Universe?

WOMAN: I don't know, it probably wouldn't matter. I expected you to talk more about your religion, about the wisdom of Buddhism, Hinduism, not about Christianity.

MONK: I don't belong to any religion. I am merely an observer of them. The only religion in the Universe is love! Buddha, Jesus, Muhammad, Krishna were just masters who showed us what we can also do by experiencing the fifth dimension right here. We happen to take more examples from Christianity because it is the largest religion in the world at the moment, and therefore many people consciously or unconsciously guide their lives according to its teachings. The ideology of Christianity is simple, isn't it? If you are a good Christian and live by respecting its faith and rituals, you will go to heaven; if not, you will go to hell. These decisions are made by a patriarchal God. Thus, to return to our topic, Christianity, Islam, Judaism, Buddhism, Hinduism, all these religions speak about the same thing. They speak about love as the absolute feeling. Most people think that our relationship with God needs mediators, priests, monks, imams. But it doesn't need mediators. It doesn't need a location either. God is neither in churches, nor in mosques, nor in temples, nor in synagogues. He is outside in the leaves of the trees, in the grains of sand. He is in everything and nothing. He is omnipresent. Go outside and see the butterflies gracefully flapping their wings. They are God. Go outside and feel the sun's rays touching your skin. They are God. Feel the waves of the sea breaking on the shore. They are God. Feel the mud between your toes. God is there. He is infinite love. So, if faith is not enough, maybe science will help in revealing spirituality. The West has already proved that love has one of the highest vibrational frequencies compared to fear, anger, shame, guilt, or apathy. While love reaches a vibration of 500 Hz, guilt, apathy and fear oscillate below 100 Hz. Love gives birth to forgiveness, compassion, gratitude, the joy of being — that authentic, unconditional joy. You can think of high-frequency emotions like matter that is not very dense — like air, for example — and low-frequency emotions are like something much denser — a large cube entirely made of metal, let's say. I think we both agree that air is much more flexible than a rigid metal cube. It's the same with these emotions you carry in life. When you act out of love, you will notice that things seem to start happening on their own. Inspiration appears from nowhere, everything around you begins to flow, like air swirling through the leaves of the trees, without any effort. On the other hand, when you act out of fear, you will notice how things seem blocked, that there's no way out, that everything seems rigid — just like the metal cube. So, all these religions I've mentioned speak about love, about enlightenment, about that supreme state that each of us can achieve. From the wisdom of the masters, we know that enlightenment is when the wave realizes it is the ocean. Beautifully put, isn't it? Enlightenment isn't something for the chosen ones, it can be achieved by anyone who chooses it.

WOMAN: Who chooses it? Do you mean manifestation, like when you want something, and the Universe responds? Though I've noticed that it doesn't always respond to our desires ....

MONK: Precisely because you want to, you will not see what you desire or you will see it very late. The Universe, which is a great catalogue with absolutely everything you have imagined and have not imagined, is very receptive to your desires and, if you are in want, it will give you exactly that, that is, the experience of "wanting." The Universe gives you what you are, not what you want. Think of these words. I repeat, the Universe doesn't give you what you want, it gives you what you are. It responds to you through the language of feeling and faith. Reality means more than what we do; it means what we are! Become exactly the things you choose to experience as your world. Choose those things consciously and experience them, feel them — "I am happy," "I am healthy," "I am prosperous," "I am a successful writer," and so on. You can even emphasize this through a firm choice: "I choose to be happy," "I choose to be healthy," "I choose to be fulfilled." All wishes are made consciously and now, at present, because there is no time other than the present. The past and the future are only illusions, and I'm not saying that merely as a metaphor.

WOMAN: Can you be more explicit? I can understand this concept of time theoretically, but somehow it seems meaningless.

MONK: Of course! Let's take a CD as an example. When you play a song from a CD and it's minute 1:11 of the song, it doesn't mean that minute 2:22 will be "the future," since the whole song already exists on the CD. Likewise, if the song is playing at minute 3:33, it doesn't mean that minute 2:22 represents the past. There is no "*here*" or "*there*." This is just an illusion of temporal and spatial separation created by religion.

WOMAN: Created by religion?

MONK: Yes! What is the most well-known prayer you know?

WOMAN: The Lord's Prayer, the *"Our Father,"* of course. I think everyone knows it. It's the most well-known prayer in the Bible.

MONK: Exactly! It's perhaps the most well-known and recited prayer in the world, said by millions of people. What does it say? Can you recite it to see what it conveys to us?

WOMAN: Of course! *"Our Father, Who art in heaven, Hallowed be Thy Name; Thy Kingdom come; Thy Will be done, on earth as it is in Heaven ..."*

MONK: Stop there! It's a beautiful prayer that expresses separation, doesn't it? *"Our Father, Who art in heaven."* We are here, and He is there, in heaven, far from us. Let's go further and see the subtle implications of separation. The idea of separation leads to the fear of loneliness. That's why loneliness is unbearable for most people, leading them to end up in disastrous, deficient relationships, whether they are romantic or friendly relationships. Moreover, separation leads to the fear of unworthiness when you feel you don't deserve anything. Why? Because God is up in heaven, next to angels and other enlightened beings, while you are here, down on earth, in an inferior state, "cast out from paradise." As long as you are separated, not up there in a higher state, you feel undeserving — you think you don't deserve any of the good things to happen to you, you don't deserve to be happy. It can even lead to you considering you don't deserve to live — all stemming from the idea of separation, deeply rooted since childhood.

WOMAN: It's incredible how vast the implications of this idea of separation are. How can we wake up from this separation?

MONK: Being aware that God is not "up there" in heaven on a cloud. He is in each of us, and this isn't just a nice metaphor. Although ancient civilizations kept telling us this for thousands of years, science has only recently proven it by decoding the message from our DNA and showing the presence of God. But, returning to our idea, the present is the only time that exists. The analogy with the CD should help you understand this. The past and the future don't exist. Now is the only time! In reality, the future is just a catalogue from which you choose an experience, whatever that might be, because all possibilities already exist. Do you remember when you were a child? You didn't know the illusion of a past or a future because children are the closest to the state of spirit. You just lived in a continuous present. Do you remember?

WOMAN: Of course, I used to play all day, jump in warm rain puddles in summer and breathe life through every pore of my skin. I miss those moments when I simply used "to be."

MONK: I understand, but you don't have to wait to return to the Source. You can experience what you are right here! That's why you chose Earth as a vacation destination with a round-trip ticket.

WOMAN: You've made me laugh. It's incredible how you always manage to see the good side of things. If the Earth were not so beautiful, with its seas and oceans, its mountains and plains, its flowers and forests, I would probably never return. It's too much trouble.

MONK: When you look back, you'll discover that it was all just a story, that nothing was truly real. So, what's stopping you from living this story as you wish?

WOMAN: I don't know. Probably the fact that our stories and our desires don't always come true.

MONK: That's because the next stage after making a conscious choice, practically a declaration to the Universe, is the moment when it must align with and pass through the three realms — the mind, the soul and the body, or the Holy Trinity, as the Christians call it.

WOMAN: Now that you mention it, what is the difference between the soul and the spirit? Aren't they the same thing?

MONK: The soul is the bridge between the spirit and the body. The spirit is the vibration, the breath of the Source. The soul appears when you choose the Trinity from the Source, that is, to think, to speak, and to act accordingly and link them to the body through your senses. Simply put, the spirit is the consciousness of God, of the Source, while the soul is your own consciousness. Therefore, assuming that desire is a conscious choice, we can already say that the realm of the mind is reached. The other two realms remain to be attained. Although the mind wants something, the soul may not agree. So, make sure they are on the same wavelength. How? Feel! Look inside yourself and feel if that desire, that story, is also the desire and story of your soul. If they aren't the same, you won't get that thing, or you'll get it with great difficulty and feel miserable throughout life, forcing your body to go where your soul doesn't want to. You've probably noticed such situations in the business world, where some people enter businesses just for money, a mental desire, without having the soul's desire. Then they either fail at some point, give up along the way, or work so hard that they end up at a point where an illness or accident occurs. The soul's desire is probably one of the most important ones. It provides the energy, the fuel of the desire. The soul's desire is what propels its manifestation in the three-dimensional world. Thus, there are people who work in their businesses with exuberant energy, with endless enthusiasm. In their cases, the mind and the soul are on the same wavelength, and their energy makes the body act accordingly. In other words, a mental desire alone is not enough, and this is perfectly normal and healthy. Just imagine if all people's mental desires became a reality in the next second. Everything would be chaos. So, I could choose to have the latest luxury car model, the mind says yes, but do I really want it? Does the soul really want this? The answer is no, so the body won't have the energy, the fuel, the emotion necessary to embody the desire.

WOMAN: But what if the answer isn't always clear and oscillates?

MONK: Then leave your mind and let your soul speak. Ask yourself if the answer is an affirmation of what you choose to be. Your soul understands what the mind cannot conceive.

WOMAN: But what if I don't have time to listen to my soul and I need a quick, immediate answer?

MONK: Then the answer is no. At least at that moment in time, it's a "no." If it's not a clear "yes," then it's a definite "no."

WOMAN: Could it be a solution to wait for a period of time to see if that desire remains as strong or if it was just something transitory? Of course, this would apply to decisions that don't require an immediate answer.

MONK: Of course. There's no such thing as a single solution to a problem. Use what you feel suits you. Just look around, and you'll notice there are countless solutions for anything you consider to be a "problem." You can learn the most important lessons and find solutions even from seemingly trivial things like a piece of chewing gum.

Chapter 6

The Wisdom of Chewing Gum

WOMAN: I don't think I have anything to learn from a piece of chewing gum.

MONK: Really? What if we all learned from it to be as flexible and malleable in life, instead of being so rigid in our thinking and feelings? Even after it loses its flavor, whether sweet or minty (much like the wonderful moments in our lives) it still remains just as flexible and malleable as it ever was. Most problems would be solved if only we applied the wisdom of chewing gum. So, you can learn something from anyone and anything. Buddhist wisdom teaches us that if we deeply observe, everything is a teacher. From the elements of nature — earth, water, fire, and air — we learn the most important lessons. The earth teaches us how to control matter, medicine, and plants. Water, the element of information, teaches us how to control the information in DNA, blood, and everything within our cells. Fire, represented by the heart, teaches us how to control the information of the spirit and emotions, and how to alter reality through fire. Air teaches us everything about the Universe, about how everything is connected. You can learn important things even from the most unexpected people — they can be the revealers of new ideas. Additionally, you can learn a lot of things from the surrounding nature. You just have to be open, to see and to hear beyond your senses, through every cell in your body, not just through your eyes and ears. Over decades, I have learned so many lessons from the mountains that surround us. The Himalayas have been and continue to be one of the best masters I could have.

WOMAN: Can we go through these lessons? I'm sure each lesson has its wisdom, just as the chewing gum does.

MONK: Of course. Let's start with the first lesson. Carrying a load that was too heavy for me during a journey to Zham, I learned that, just like in our everyday life, we often carry burdens and resentments that are too heavy for us. "*Those free of resentment are the ones who will find peace,*" says the great Buddha. So, remember that it's crucial to let go of the unnecessary baggage to travel freely through life.

WOMAN: An interesting lesson! I'll write it down.

MONK: The next lesson came from observing all the climbers from around the world who come every year to conquer Chomolungma.

WOMAN: Do you mean Mount Everest, the highest in the world?

MONK: For us, it's Chomolungma, which means Mother of the Universe. For our brothers in Nepal, it's Sagarmatha, which means Mother of the Ocean, but we will use the term Everest, as it is known to Westerners, if it's easier for you. So, the lesson, watching the thousands of climbers from all corners of the world who want to conquer Mount Everest every year, comes as a question: do you really want to reach Mount Everest, or is it just a trophy to add to the list of peaks you've conquered? Is it a desire of the soul or just a trend? This question leads to deep introspection. You see, in life we often do things just because "we have to," because "that's the way things are done," because "that's the way things work" or to "prove something to others," and that's where most problems begin. You'll notice this, if you haven't already, in a lot of employees. They climb the corporate ladder because they think this is the "normal" way of things. That is, until fatigue, unhappiness or even health problems show up and warn them that it's not their dream. And indeed, it's not their dream. If, just for a second, they had listened to their soul, they would have known that.

WOMAN: I understand what you mean, and you are right, indeed. There's a social pressure to do the "right things" and at the "right time." You finish your studies, now it's time to get a job. You get a job, now it's time to start a family, have children, and so on. A house and a car have become objects of social status and are part of the "must-have" category, but no one asks if you really want these things or if they truly make you happy.

MONK: I think you know these things best. Simplicity creates clarity both for the mind and for the soul. Yes, there's nothing wrong with having any material thing you want, but what is wrong is to believe that these things will truly make you happy. What is wrong is to consider that external things can bring you the happiness of being, the purest form of happiness. So, next time when a project or anything else looms on the horizon, ask yourself honestly and let the voice of the spirit whisper — do you really want to climb Everest? Or is it someone else's dream? This question has nothing to do with Everest. You see, ultimately, success is not always about reaching the peak. Sometimes, the mystery of life lies in the journey itself, between the foot and the peak of the mountain.

WOMAN: Beautiful words! Truly wonderful! I will keep in mind the wisdom of this lesson.

MONK: Ready for the next one?

WOMAN: Sure!

MONK: The next important lesson the mountains teach us is about the people around us. Climbing Everest is done alongside Sherpas. Sherpas are those people who are with you and guide you during the journey to the summit, as they have traversed it many times. However, this doesn't mean they don't risk their lives. Just like climbing mountains with the right people, it's equally important in life to be surrounded by those people with whom you can travel together. It's also important to understand that you cannot force anyone to stay in your life. Remember the scenario you wrote before coming to Earth. Nothing happens by chance. Each person in your life stays exactly as long as they need to. Some people may stay for a lifetime, while others may stay only for a few days or a few hours. Detachment is crucial here — detachment from people, pets, or objects. It doesn't mean you shouldn't own anything; it means nothing owns you. Train yourself to let go of attachments to the things you are afraid of losing. Imagine the people and the things you are attached to disappearing from your life. Detachment doesn't mean indifference or ignorance, as it is often misunderstood. Attachment is based on the fear of losing, which can often turn into dependence, jealousy, or obsession. Loving without attachments is the sublime form of love.

WOMAN: I understand what you're saying, but for most people, it's not easy to accept these things or, if someone does accept them, it's only superficially. Thus, their reality still reflects attachments and dependencies of all kinds.

MONK: Through awareness and practice, everything becomes much easier. The human mind can be trained, regardless of its current state. Remember the analogy of the spaceship that has to overcome the gravitational force to fly smoothly into space. Yes, it may take a lot of energy to achieve this, but once achieved, it will all be well worth it! Overcome the gravitational force! After that, you will be able to fly smoothly through life, without burdens.

WOMAN: A lesson full of meaning and wisdom! What is the next one?

MONK: The next lesson is about adaptability! Encountering four weather phenomena on the trails of the Himalayas — sun, rain, hail, and snow — in less than two hours, this may seem impossible, but it happens quite often in the mountains. This phenomenon made me reflect on another life lesson. You see, in life we often face the same "natural phenomena": the death of a loved one, followed by the birth of someone else, a resounding success, followed by a devastating failure. Just as you prepare with proper footwear and a raincoat for the mountains, or a hat for the scorching sun at the mountain top, you must do the same in life — to be well prepared.

WOMAN: But how? I want a raincoat against problems. In life, you can't foresee every situation so as to be fully prepared for anything that might come up.

MONK: It's not about foreseeing or controlling every detail of your life, but there are certain aspects for which it's important to be prepared, such as death. Death is perhaps the only certainty we have in this life.

WOMAN: But I wouldn't like to talk about death! I think it's a very sad and depressing topic.

MONK: Indeed! That's why we will talk about it a little later, as it's a broad topic. For now, to be prepared for life, it's worth training yourself. Remember what you are! Train your mind, spirit and body every day. This is the Holy Triad or the Holy Trinity for Christians. There are tens of thousands of ancient Tibetan writings discussing these three realms. Discussing each of them would take forever, but we will summarize them as much as possible and give some accessible and easy-to-apply advice. Let's begin with the mind. The mind is like a sponge. This is where most of the subconscious patterns accumulated throughout life lie. It absorbs everything, whether you are aware of it or not. Feed it with quality information — from books to productive discussions with the people around you, and start cleaning out those mental patterns that no longer serve you. This is done through awareness. Awareness means awakening. It's the "Aha!" moment. Once you've had your first moment of awareness, you won't stop until you accumulate more and more. This is how a strong mind is built. Remember, it's never about the problems. They don't even exist in a state of neutrality. Something that's a problem for you may be an opportunity for someone else. It's an opportunity because they've trained themselves to see it this way. You see, let's assume we assess a "problem" on a scale of 1 to 10, where 1 means the problem has no impact and it can hardly be considered a problem, and 10 means it has the greatest impact. You will notice the following: if now you assess someone's betrayal as a 10, meaning that it has a devastating impact on you, later on, after sufficiently working with yourself and raising your awareness, you will assess this "problem" as a 3 or maybe a 1, which means it has no impact on you. Conversely, if you don't engage in growth, in awareness and sink deeper into pain, then you will assess this "problem" as a 10,000. So, the "problem" is never about the "problem." It's not external. You see external things as they are reflected by your own interior. Look out the front window. What do you see?

WOMAN: I see the snowy mountains in the distance, the sun caressing the rooftops of houses, and the local people walking on the road. Why?

MONK: Now look out the window behind you. What do you see?

WOMAN: Not much. It's dirty and dusty, probably because of the rain. I can barely see a few moving shadows. It needs cleaning.

MONK: Exactly! The external reality is the same. The window through which you look makes the difference between seeing either the beauty or the filth around you. Clean the window of the dirt in your life and you will see the external beauty of this world.

Chapter 7

Chomolungma's Lessons

WOMAN: So, our exterior world is always reflected by our interior world, and not the other way around. And although we know this, most of the time we don't take it into account.

MONK: Both of your statements are correct.

WOMAN: But why do we do it? If we know these things that would make our lives so much easier, why don't we apply them?

MONK: Because it takes faith. There we are, back to this aspect. To put into practice the things we aspire to, we need a brave spirit, and a brave spirit cannot exist without faith — faith in the Universe, in God, in what you truly are. Each of us is a Universe, and when you realize this and faith fills every pore of your skin, you will notice how, through a simple conscious choice, you will begin to move forward in small but consistent steps. It doesn't matter how slowly you move on, as long as you don't stop. The mountains also offer you this lesson. Year after year, I see climbers from all corners of the world rushing to reach Everest, ignoring the importance of small steps and hurrying like in a marathon on the steep ridges. They don't realize that small steps mean less energy consumed because fewer muscle fibers are engaged, so the body and muscles need less oxygen. Small steps also mean stability. So, in their rush, most climbers already begin to get tired, and their bodies start to give out. The luckiest of them go back, but the others end up in the arms of fatigue and cold with a lack of oxygen.

WOMAN: That's because the mountain always takes its toll.

MONK: The mountain takes no toll. The sea takes no toll. There's no such thing. It's like saying that the mountain is something mighty that takes revenge whenever it feels like it. The same image you have created about God. Don't you see that you are endlessly perpetuating the same patterns? The same dirty window you keep looking through.

WOMAN: But that's what people say! Every time someone dies on the mountain, you will hear people say that "the mountain took its toll."

MONK: And you simply chose to blindly believe this? Did you pass it through your filter of truth? Just because I, your parents, your family, or anyone else who is "experienced" or works in one field or another says something, it doesn't mean you should take it for granted without passing it through your own filter.

WOMAN: What do you mean by this filter?

MONK: This filter is your soul, your spirit. Listen to it! Listen to its whispered voice trying to reach to you!

WOMAN: Do you mean intuition?

MONK: Some call it intuition. You will notice that, although sometimes the mind can offer you the most valid arguments that contradict intuition, in the end, the mind's arguments are invalidated, and intuition wins every time. That's why it's important to listen to it. It may be hard at first, but as I said, with practice, everything is possible. At first, the mind, which is here for survival, will deny that inner voice because the mind wants survival, while the spirit wants expansion. So, returning to the actual lesson, small steps and consistency are very important. Long term consistency beats short-term intensity, right? The great Einstein probably said it best: *"Compound interest is the eighth wonder of the world. He who understands it, earns it. He who doesn't, pays it."* Just reflect on these words and think about all the areas of your life where you apply or don't apply this principle. Do you think most relationships of any kind end abruptly, suddenly? Not at all. They end because a misunderstanding happening a few months before wasn't clarified; because a misunderstanding happening a few weeks or days before wasn't looked into and nothing was learned from it. You see, this is how the compound effect the great physicist talks about is paid. On the other hand, today's wonderful state of health, the exceptional physical shape, is not the result of what you did two minutes ago, but of what you have been doing in recent years, in recent months — the earned compound effect.

WOMAN: In other words, if I saved a dollar every day, I might not see a luxury car in my garage in two days, but after a few years of saving, I might see it.

MONK: Beautiful! You know what you want in life, although it all might end up like in *"Monk Who Sold His Ferrari"** . However, it seems that you understand how this effect works, what small but consistent steps can mean in every area of our lives. Small steps build stability, but it's important to remember that this applies in both directions.

WOMAN: I understand. Small steps meaning that today you

---

* Robin Sharma's book, in which a great lawyer from New York sold his Ferrari and everything he owned to dedicate himself to the search for wisdom and the meaning of life.

smoke, drink excessively, eat unhealthy food, have unhealthy habits and thoughts, and that will bring you to that point where the body will give out due to either illness or even death. On the other hand, if you consistently practice sports, eat healthily, have noble thoughts and feelings of love, compassion, gratitude, you will reach that point where you will earn the compound effect of these habits. Or, more simply put, if I save a dollar today, in a few years I will have a luxury car in my garage. Am I right? Don't laugh!

MONK: I'm not laughing, I'm just amused! It's always a pleasure to meet crazy Western people in search of the meaning of life.

WOMAN: It's strange how I felt love and compassion in those words.

MONK: Jokes, humor, irony, sarcasm are part of the expression of divinity. God indeed has a sense of humor and you will notice this quite often if you look around you. Life is a game, not a war. Ultimately, it's what you choose it to be, but if you choose to see it as a game, you will notice the beauty of life just like children do. For them, everything is a game, everything is love, joy, and enthusiasm. We think we bring children into this world to teach them, but what really happens is that they teach us. No adult has the faith, innocence and purity of a child. That's why it's important to make plans in life like an adult and believe in their achievement like a child.

WOMAN: Interesting advice! It's probably true. I've noticed that things go much easier for those people who don't take life so seriously, who are smiling and always kind.

MONK: Try it and you will see.

WOMAN: So, what other lessons have you learned from the mountains?

MONK: On one of the journeys to Lhasa, a terrible snowstorm started and we couldn't see anything in front of our eyes. We all insisted to keep going despite the weather, but at one point I made the decision to go back. What do you think the lesson is?

WOMAN: I don't know. I thought it wasn't right to give up, no matter what happened. It seemed that you really wanted to get there, so it wasn't a question of whether you wanted to reach the destination or not.

MONK: Exactly! I wanted to get there. The lesson from that journey to Lhasa, in the midst of a severe snowstorm, is about the wisdom of knowing when to continue and when to give up. The decision to go further, despite the dangerous conditions, can be seen as a demonstration of perseverance and determination, but also as a great risk. Going back at the right moment shows the wisdom of recognizing own limits and prioritizing the safety of others and of yourself in a potentially dangerous situation. It's a lesson of discernment when confronted with nature's adversities and the importance of listening to intuition and of continuously assessing the situation to make the best decisions on a journey. In the end, you don't conquer the mountain, you conquer yourself.

WOMAN: But how did you realize it was time to give up for the moment and return later?

MONK: I listened to my spirit, my inner voice. It told me it was time to go back and return another day.

WOMAN: And did you return?

MONK: Of course! After two weeks of constant blizzard, we set out again and reached our destination. You see, rerouting is often seen as a sign of weakness, of giving up, but remember that it's important to always write your dream with a pen and your path with a pencil, because most of the time you will often use the pencil eraser to retrace a new path to your dream.

WOMAN: This sounds like that incident when a woman missed her flight, and shortly afterwards that plane crashed. Apparently, a "bad" thing for her turned into a life-saving event.

MONK: Exactly! It's very important to be flexible in life, not to resist. Water teaches us this lesson very well by taking the shape of its container. It always knows its purpose in life. Thus, rerouting doesn't mean giving up but finding another way to reach the destination. Many times, this can be a much easier path than the one we initially chose. You have to let the Universe guide you and not resist. Be in flow with life, and an apparently "bad" thing can turn into the blessing of your life. Let me tell you a revealing story in this regard. It is said that, once upon a time, a farmer lived at the northern border of China. One day, his horse ran away. All the people in the village where he lived felt sorry him, saying: "Oh, what bad luck, your horse ran away!" But the farmer replied calmly: "Maybe bad luck, maybe good luck.... Who knows?" After a while, the farmer's only son climbed on one of the two wild horses, trying to tame it. The horse got scared and threw the boy off, who broke his leg. The villagers, full of compassion, told the farmer: "What bad luck, your only son broke his leg!" The farmer replied as calmly as always: "Maybe bad luck, maybe good luck.... Who knows?" A few months later, a great war broke out. All the young men in the village went to war, except the farmer's son who wasn't sent to the battlefield due to his broken leg. This story teaches us that events in life can seem negative or positive, depending on perspective. What seems like bad luck at first can turn into good luck or vice versa. True wisdom lies in allowing ourselves to be carried by the flow of life and seeing each experience as part of our unique journey.

WOMAN: Indeed, the story is eye-opening. We should probably be much more open to life. So, what other lessons have you inferred from the wisdom of the mountains?

MONK: Gratitude as a general state of being, gratitude for the entire existence. Before and after a journey, I am always grateful to the mountains for guiding me along the steep paths, for allowing me to see the beauty that surrounds them, even if there were cases when I suffered an injury or I had to go back before reaching the destination.

WOMAN: Why should we be grateful for the bad things in our lives?

MONK: Because as I said before, there are no "good" or "bad" things at a higher level. Yes, in the relative world where we are, they exist, but do they really exist?

WOMAN: I'm confused ....

MONK: We've just talked about these aspects. If an accident of any kind or a fracture on the mountain saved you from a rockslide in which you could have lost your life, could it still be considered a "bad" thing? If missing a train, which is apparently a "bad" thing because you need to reach your destination, saved you from the derailment of that train into the depths of the valleys, could it still be considered a bad thing? Indeed, we can sometimes see the good part of such events, but most of the time we don't recognize it at the moment. An accident that leaves a deep scar now can lead to a conversation with a stranger on a train five years later, a conversation that can turn into a lifelong marriage. You see, we don't always immediately understand or see the good hidden behind the "bad," but it's always there and we must have faith in this. After all, we deserve everything that happens to us because we are the ones who write the script of our lives. So, be grateful for everything that happens in your life, whether it's "good" or "bad." A marriage that ends, a missed train, an accident or an illness — all these can hide a higher good, which our mind cannot always perceive. Therefore, it's important to be open to life, not to resist things, to be flexible and adaptable, like the chewing gum in its wisdom.

Chapter 8

Free Spirits Set Others Free

WOMAN: I understand. You're right, but it's often difficult to see this, especially in interpersonal relationships, whether we're talking about a marriage, workplace relationships, or any other kind of social interactions.

MONK: Indeed! Interpersonal relationships are among the Universe's favorite ways of reminding us of the most important lessons. Let's take a classic example. Suppose Charlotte and Daniel make a wonderful couple, but they start to argue. Charlotte reacts impulsively when Daniel tells her that her cooking needs more salt. She feels criticized and reacts aggressively, raising her voice and striking back. Daniel tells Charlotte that she doesn't love him and doesn't care about his feelings because she doesn't immediately respond to his messages or phone calls.

WOMAN: A perfectly normal relationship.

MONK: I appreciate your irony, as I've told you before. Now let's analyze this scenario. If Daniel realized that his reaction is nothing but a pattern from when his mother wasn't around, and he felt unloved and abandoned, the situation would change. Similarly, if Charlotte realized that her aggressive reaction to criticism is just a pattern from when her father wasn't satisfied with her grades and she couldn't please him, the situation would change. Both of them would take the first and most important step towards healing — awareness. We keep coming back to it and its importance because, ultimately, awareness means awakening! It's crucial for healing and fulfillment. So, both Daniel and Charlotte are reacting automatically based on old patterns from their childhood when their inner child was hurt. The inner child is essentially the subconscious. Your science has already discovered some of its characteristics, but the most important thing is that it represents a substantial part of the human brain, while the rational part — the adult — represents only a small part. Knowing this, you can easily see that the inner child will always lead the course of life, whether you are aware of it or not.

WOMAN: In this sense, Daniel and Charlotte's separation seems imminent, or is at least one of the possible solutions.

MONK: It can be a solution, but not necessarily a good one, because even if Charlotte and Daniel decide to go their separate ways, they will encounter the same patterns of partners who will reactivate the same wounds. They won't get rid of their problems, they will only postpone them. However, if both consciously choose not to run away and to heal those wounds, the situation will change.

WOMAN: Or maybe both of them could simply control those impulses.

MONK: It's not about controlling those impulses or "anesthetizing emotions." This might work temporarily, but in the long run, it can lead to real catastrophes: depression, suicide, or murder. I mentioned that the "adult," the conscious mind, represents only a small percentage of this equation. Do you think it can control the subconscious, which accounts for about 80-90% of the human mind?

WOMAN: Probably not. So, what can be done?

MONK: As I said, the first step is the conscious choice, where both partners decide to solve these problems together. The second step is the awareness of the main cause of the problem. I say the main cause, meaning the pattern, the trauma in the subconscious. You can't treat the sick leaves of an apple tree until you understand the cause, which might be represented by a worm or an insect, right? When they become aware of the real problem, then Daniel will understand that if Charlotte doesn't immediately answer the phone, it doesn't mean she doesn't love him. And Charlotte will understand that Daniel made a simple observation, not a criticism that warrants a violent reaction.

WOMAN: An interesting approach to things and, at the same time, frightening if you think that this is just an example from a social environment that wouldn't have such a significant impact. Just think of those people who lead countries or are at the top of leadership, and of their impact on society if they have such unhealed wounds. This leads to dictators or power-hungry people who drag entire countries into unnecessary wars.

MONK: I believe we've already thought about this, as we've already lived and are living the reality of it. We can extend the example of Daniel and Charlotte into various areas, for instance, in the relationship between a boss and an employee, where the boss is seen as a "dictator" by the employee. When the employee decides to search for and become aware of those traumas in the subconscious — maybe an overly authoritarian parent who didn't allow him to go out of the house or do certain activities — he will "suddenly" notice that the boss has changed. All of a sudden, the boss is no longer so "dictatorial" and authoritarian but has become a true leader. Of course, what has changed is not the boss, but the perspective from which he or she is seen after healing and awareness have occurred. Most of the times, these changes happen as soon as awareness has taken place, so don't be surprised by the radical changes that appear around you. Indeed, there may also be "reality changes" that take place more slowly, but most of them will happen quickly once awareness has occurred. So, returning to our topic and concluding, since we started talking about gratitude as a lesson, it's very important to be grateful and open both to "good" and "bad" things, but especially to "bad" ones, because that's where the most important lessons lie.

WOMAN: I understand and it really makes sense. What do these hand signs that you're making mean?

MONK: It's a mudra. We often use it in conversation with others, but there are dozens of mudras you can use. Mudra is a seal, a kind of holy cross that Christians make when they worship. You can look at it this way.

WOMAN: It looks like witchcraft. I thought you were also a witch. Even to this day, magic is considered occult, demonic, and is seen as something unclean.

MONK: Magic is just energy. It is seen by some as occult because they fear it. And what do people fear? What they don't understand. Magic is just energy manipulated in a constructive or destructive way. It's been preached as something unholy to hide its power, a power that each of us have and can activate. Most consider it "evil" because they don't understand it, and more often than not, what is not understood is denied. Just think about it. Magic is used to treat everything from physical ailments to trauma to unresolved emotions. Shamans know this best by using herbs and alternative medicine for healing. So why would this be a bad thing? Astrology, the zodiac, is again something seen by some religions as something unholy, therefore it is forbidden. Why? The twelve zodiac signs represent portals, guides since ancient times. They are star alignments on the mirror of the Universe, and we are stardust. Isn't it strange that everything that represents our true nature is considered "demonic" or "unholy"? Indeed, magic can be used in the form of charms to make someone fall in love with you, for example. Yes, we are talking about its destructive power here, because it is not good to violate someone's free will. So, magic is not something good or bad, as we talked about under the potentiality of things. In short, it's not good to violate someone else's free will, because we are violating the laws of the Universe.

WOMAN: But what about helping others? How do you know you're not violating their free will by helping them?

MONK: How do you think you could figure it out?

WOMAN: I don't know, that's why I asked.

MONK: What opens the mind is the question, not the answer. You are here to bring awareness to the question. The question makes you create. You will have to answer the question yourself: why do you wish to help them? To hide some unrecognized trauma by which you feel validated or because you deliberately, without attachment, want to contribute to a better world? Further, there is a fine line between helping and violating free will. You see, sometimes, no matter what you do, some people don't want to be "rescued," which is perfectly normal. Everyone is exactly where they need to be at the moment! Remember that! In other words, by whatever means you try to wake up, to help a person, if metaphorically speaking their goal is to hit their head against the wall, then they will do so, even if you put a pillow to stop them from hitting themselves against it. So, if you violate someone's free will, the Universe has countless ways to get out of their way. Either another high-priority issue comes out of nowhere that you need to deal with, or you'll have to move. There are countless ways that the Universe gets you out of the way. You can't imagine the infinity of the ways it has. So, the answer lies within you. Your soul already knows it. Listen to it through every pore.

WOMAN: What if I want and feel like helping a beggar and he uses the money for something else, like buying alcohol or cigarettes instead of food?

MONK: The answer is already in your question. Once you want and feel to do something, you live according to the *True You*. It is not your business what happens next. Further, it is the responsibility of the one who has received what you have given. He will live with what he has done.

WOMAN: Interesting perspective! Then, if I wanted and felt like helping him, but didn't, I would have had trouble living with what I failed to do, because I didn't live according to the *True Self*, right?

MONK: Exactly!

WOMAN: But are there other ways we can help those around us?

MONK: There are indeed solutions. The simplest is to be that change you want to see around you. In this way, you will help others without directly helping them. In other words, you help them without making any conscious effort. After all, inaction is still an action that can change the world.

WOMAN: I don't understand. It doesn't make sense. Could you elaborate?

MONK: Compassion is the answer. Compassion is what connects all things. Compassion is the force of the Universe. Compassion doesn't mean pity. We often make that mistake. Compassion is being passionate about something, right? That's the origin of the word. Compassion means sharing passion, sharing happiness for creation. Christianity teaches that this compassion means helping others. But others are a projection of us, right? The only way to help others is if you are in balance and in coherence with yourself. Then, acting from this state of coherence and balance, you share your passion with others. So, others can wake up and see that you are fine with you because you are focused on yourself. Great, isn't it?

WOMAN: I never thought about this perspective of seeing things.

MONK: Come back into harmony, into balance with yourself, experience the passion of creation, everything around you and notice how things around you are changing. This is a promise! You don't have to take my word for it. In fact, no master will ever ask you to take his word for it. Just experience the power of compassion and see how everything around you begins to change. The more you nurture and experience compassion, the more you will see people around you awakening, healing, blossoming. This is how you help others without helping them directly. Interesting, isn't it? Be the light of the candle. The flame of a candle can light the candles around it. Be what you want to see around you, and reality will change by itself, effortlessly. When you are light to yourself, you are light to others. You see, people who are hurt also hurt other people, but healed people heal other people. Awakened people awaken other people. Free spirits set others free. Putting yourself first is not selfishness. Putting yourself first and discovering who you really are is the greatest gift you can give yourself and others. Once you choose you, everything else will choose you.

WOMAN: But in a couple relationship, this might seem selfish because you're not thinking about the one next to you. It's seen as showing carelessness or insensitivity.

MONK: Putting yourself first is not a sign of selfishness, carelessness, or ignorance. No matter how harsh this may sound, the truth is that you are not here to be responsible for anyone else's happiness, whether we're talking about your partner, parents, or even your children! Imagine yourself as a battery. If you are empty, without energy, how can you help others or be close to them? The goal is to always have a full battery, and this is possible when you are connected to Source. How do you think you can create a harmonious relationship with others if you have not first created a harmonious relationship with yourself? Your willingness to help is a wonderful quality. You can continue to manifest it. But the more you help yourself, the more you can help others. That is the power of compassion!

WOMAN: It seems there's a reason they say to put your oxygen mask first in an airplane in case of an emergency.

MONK: How else could you help others if you didn't!

Chapter 9

LGBTQ+, Addictions, and Monkeys

WOMAN: Indeed! Now can we talk about addictions? I have noticed that it is a sensitive and often painful subject.

MONK: Of course. Addictions of any kind — from alcohol, smoking, food, addiction to other people or even a sport — all reflect an inner emptiness that is trying to be satisfied with something on the outside, which is insane. The more we distance ourselves from our inner selves, from who we really are, the emptier we become inside. In this state, we strive to fill this inner emptiness with various external things.

WOMAN: Addiction to a sport? But why. Sport and movement, in general, is good for our body.

MONK: Because addiction simply talks about hiding pain, in one form or another. Just ask yourself honestly and answer as honestly, "Why do you do that sport?" To celebrate what the human body can do, or to hide a pain, a breakup, or maybe it's a punishment to your body because you overeat? Notice the difference in purpose?

Of course, if you compare them, a sports addiction is much more beneficial than an alcohol addiction, but it's still an addiction after all.

WOMAN: Even the shopping addiction?

MONK: Even this. Addiction to anything and in any form speaks of hiding the misery within, of compensating for it with something physical from the outside.

WOMAN: I bring it up because on the surface you wouldn't see it as an addiction, but one of my friends has this shopping addiction. As absurd as it sounds, she can't stop herself from shopping constantly. Her psychologist told her to keep shopping. How crazy is that?

MONK: We cannot know what that psychologist meant or what technique he or she applied. We're not here to judge. Indeed, we should be careful about the "specialists" we turn to, because some want to get you addicted to them through countless sessions or other methods, thinking only about profit first and foremost, without understanding how things work. The goal of a mentor or therapist for every soul should be to help them to be complete and independent, not to make them dependent on them. That is not the goal, to become dependent on someone to ensure your healing in any form. A true mentor understands this and gives the mentee all the tools to be able to heal himself or herself, to become self-sufficient, no matter what the circumstances. That is the ultimate goal. After all, that was the goal of Jesus in Christianity, as it was the goal of any other teacher in other religions. They didn't want us to depend on them, but to see what we too can do like them. Again, no judgment.

WOMAN: But we are not judging anyone. It's an objective reality. I understand that you're in that stage of wisdom where everything is milk and honey, but I think we're in a time when psychologists need psychologists. I wouldn't want to generalize, but in most cases this is true. How do you think it's possible that after years of therapy, common symptoms don't improve? I'm not talking about cure, I'm talking about improvement, and after gaining the knowledge of the old wisdom, for the healing to take place? That is why I am here, because neither religion nor classical psychology has been able to answer some fundamental questions. Damn it! Fundamental questions! Yes, the West has technology, but the East has wisdom! What good is it to have all the technology in the world if inside you feel empty?

MONK: It's okay, I understand your frustration!

WOMAN: I don't know if you understand. You're not in the middle of things, trapped like a hamster wheel, running endlessly in a cage called "life."

MONK: Do you think it would help if we took a break? Try taking a sip of tea and deep breaths. This will help.

WOMAN: It's okay, we can continue. Sorry!

MONK: There is nothing to forgive! It's okay to let what you're feeling come out, to allow yourself to be vulnerable, and then to analyse those emotions.

WOMAN: To be vulnerable?! You've gotta be kidding! You'd be squashed like a bug by society in those moments of "vulnerability."

MONK: That's because you perpetuate subconscious "strongest wins" patterns in which emotion means weakness. You teach Darwin's "origin of the species" as the ultimate reference in schools, even though dozens of writings have invalidated those theories.

WOMAN: How do you know these things?

MONK: I would give you a simple answer: you already know these things inside you, you feel them, but I know that the rational part of you is looking for a much more exact answer. We could look at some old Tibetan scriptures in the old library, but I'm sure that deciphering the ancient teachings from manuscripts that barely hold their words on paper is not your goal at this point. So, there is another solution that's within anyone's reach. There are countless books that have already dealt with decrypting these manuscripts. In Gregg Braden's *"Human by Design: From Evolution by Chance to Transformation by Choice,"* a wonderful man who has spent part of his life in these places, you'll find the answer to your question about why "origin of species" is no longer supported by hard evidence. Yet it is still taught in schools.

WOMAN: And what's wrong with that, after all?

MONK: Everything! You live your whole life thinking you evolved randomly from monkeys. What are the consequences of these beliefs? The fact that you live as if everything is chaos, that everything happens by "chance," randomly, chaotically, without having a say in things, without knowing that you are created with intent, that everything around you has an order, that there is nothing random.

WOMAN: So?

MONK: This leads you to either live your life in despair or in helplessness, because you have imprinted in your subconscious that everything is evolution and you have no control. Or, you could live your life with intent, with excitement and fulfillment, knowing that you were created with intent and that you can shape life in the same way — consciously, intentionally. We have said that the main purpose of the Universe is evolution, and indeed it is, but we don't mean "the strongest wins" or "in order for someone to win, someone else has to lose." Biological evolution is different from spiritual evolution. These conceptions lead to division and take you away from who you really are. Now do you see the causality of things?

WOMAN: Unbelievable!

MONK: This is exactly the reaction when you find out who you really are! Just think about the precision of the Universe. If gravity was just a little stronger, the Universe would collapse. If gravity was less strong than it is, then there would be no stars and planets in the Universe. If the relationship between certain forces wasn't as precise as it is, then life wouldn't exist. This makes you realize that nothing is random, that everything is created in detail, with intent. In no way are you a monkey! You can let others who are not ready for this truth believe this. Even they will find out the truth at some point, because it is not a matter of "if," but "when."

WOMAN: But even Stephen Hawking, the great scientist, said we are "just an advanced breed of monkeys."

MONK: I came back once more and I will come back as often as needed in this conversation. Are you living the *True You*? Have you put those words through your own filter or have you simply accepted them? Did you feel like a monkey when you managed to consciously heal yourself when the doctors failed to diagnose your pain? Do you think that people who consciously heal from cancer, despite the hopelessness of doctors, consider themselves monkeys? Do you think that people who achieve astonishing performances in sport or in any other field, consider themselves monkeys?

WOMAN: Absolutely not! I would never have thought that there could be so many implications in the fact that we believe so much in evolutionary theory.

MONK: This is only a small part. Another problematic thing is that, having ingrained the evolutionary model, you know and believe in the supremacy of the strongest, that "the best wins," that in order to "survive" you must be stronger, richer, better than the other. Then the greatest decadence begins, in which you believe that you are separate and you no longer act out of unity, but out of separation, out of ego — "for me to win, the other must lose." Why do you think some people lose their lives jumping off different constructions, trying to prove that they can fly and that they are like God? Because they are not acting out of unity, but out of separation. They say "look what I can do that you can't." When he walked on water, Jesus said "look what I can do, we all can do it." For an evolved being there is no notion of gain or loss, because they live in communion, in unity. We are one and at the same time we are many. We are many and at the same time we are one. We are not in competition with other souls. Each soul evolves at its own pace, and a soul that completes its journey is worth as much as a soul at the beginning of its journey. There is no race or competition, it is just a journey in which we are all moving toward growth and evolution. The problem comes when we don't remember who we really are beyond our physical bodies, because then the illusions and delusions of this world become much more prominent.

WOMAN: Yes, because we are taught that power, prestige, money are the things that bring us happiness, so they become the very purpose of life. We are taught that to be happy we have to be liked by others, that being alone is a terrible thing. We end up judging each other without understanding that it is normal to have different values and beliefs.

MONK: Indeed! Therefore, remembering who we really are beyond these labels, that we are immortal, that we are eternal souls, is the key to true happiness.

WOMAN: In relation to who we are, what do you think about the LGBTQ+ movement? I know it's a touchy subject, but I worked up the courage to ask anyway. Some people think that they have angered God and that's why the climate has changed and we're having global warming. Why are you laughing?

MONK: Sorry, I couldn't help myself. Some interpretations of global events are hilarious. Even us old Tibetan monks laugh. Even a lama laughs. It's funny how taking responsibility is not really among our qualities. So, we come back. I will repeat as often as need be that

God is not vengeful. He does not impose punishment. He has no preferences. When you understand that the Divine Intelligence, God, has no preferences, you will have the answer to all your questions. Love can be expressed in innumerable ways. It is not for you, me, or anyone to judge anything. Everyone has chosen their own scenario which they play out, that may or may not be related to other people's scenarios. If one has chosen such a marriage, so be it. If one has chosen monogamy, so be it. If one has chosen to be single for life, so be it. Everyone has chosen their own role and script.

WOMAN: What about climate change?

MONK: What about it? You forget that we are in communion with nature, in communion with this planet. What does communion mean? Simple! You inhale oxygen and exhale carbon dioxide. Plants need carbon dioxide and give out oxygen. See the perfection of communion? Plants need something that would harm you, but is good for them. You need what hurts them, but is good for you. It's a win-win. What is happening is that, year after year, nature is being poisoned by all kinds of pollutants, by massive exploitation, by huge deforestation due to greed. Basically, we cut our own throat or, in this case, I should say we cut down our own oxygen.

WOMAN: Maybe if greed solved the most basic needs, it would be good, but it doesn't. Millions of people die every day around the world from hunger, while, paradoxically, tons of food is thrown away.

MONK: You said it, not me. So, why would people in the LGBTQ+ community bear the blame for that? It's simply human conscience.

WOMAN: That's because most of them are so selfish and only think about their own survival.

MONK: Selfish perhaps, but the purpose of the spirit is not survival. You are free of the concept of survival because you know you will never die, only transcend. If that were so, then a random stranger would not throw himself into the water to save a child, knowing that there is a likelihood of drowning himself. The purpose of the spirit is to know the expansion of what love is in all its forms. The purpose of the mind is survival, which is beneficial when you may be attacked by a wild animal and react accordingly, but when survival becomes a permanent defence, this should give us pause for thought. So, survival is only an illusion because death itself is an illusion. Everything is an illusion. You see, most people are worried that, because technology has evolved so much, we will no longer distinguish between the real and the imaginary, but what is real? The reality we live in is not really a reality.

WOMAN: What about fear?

MONK: What about it? You choose to believe in it, so you act accordingly, based on fear. "Blessed is everyone that feareth the Lord," that's what the Bible, one of the greatest Christian scriptures, says, and you've chosen to trust those words without putting them through your own filter.

WOMAN: I know you're right, but it's not always easy not to act out of fear. There are so many patterns linked to it in the subconscious ....

Chapter 10

The Greatest Fear of All

MONK: Having talked about fear, I think it's time to talk about the greatest fear of all — death.

WOMAN: Do you have to?

MONK: Of course! The things you fear are worth understanding. The more you run from them, the more they will haunt you. The important thing to remember is that no one leaves here without choosing to. You decide when you come or go. If you feel you have nothing left to learn in this physical form, then you will leave, regardless of modern medicine. No one and nothing will stop the soul from leaving this world if it has decided that its mission here is over. After all, it doesn't have to be anything spectacular. The heart can stop without the body suffering any illness. Quite simply, without doing any complex action, the heart stops permanently and the soul leaves the body. On the other hand, if the soul feels that it still has more to learn, it can return from a deep coma or even from a near-death experience to which modern medicine has given no chance.

WOMAN: Who was near death? I don't understand. Once you're declared dead by the doctors, there's nothing they can do.

MONK: I mean, you can come back from the dead. I told you that these things do not take account of medicine, however modern. So, you can be pronounced dead by doctors. Your heart has stopped. You have no pulse. All this only to wake up hours later in a coroner's refrigerator or in a coffin next to your family who mourns you. These things have happened and they're not isolated cases. Just a few years ago, I was involved in one such experience where a "dead man" started blinking, shocked to wake up at his own funeral. From modern medicine's perspective, he was pronounced dead, but the spirit doesn't take these things into account. These things are not subject to the restrictions of science as we know it. If the soul decides that its life in this body is not over, then one way or another it will return to the body.

WOMAN: And what happened to that person who was resurrected?

MONK: He lived a few more years, then he left that body for good. You see, the accounts of these events are incredibly consistent, regardless of religion or other particulars. People detach themselves from the physical body and begin to float away, watching doctors' efforts to resuscitate them. They feel no pain. Just a pleasant sensation of relief, peace, and harmony. Then they see a bright, spiritual entity telling them that their time has not yet come. Then, they are reunited with the physical body and begin to feel pain or other physical sensations. You see, the feeling of relief, peace, and harmony when the soul is detached from the body is due to the fact that this is the nature of the spirit. It is not accustomed to experience the limitations of being imprisoned in a physical body. That is why there's sleep and dreams. Sleep is the soul's way of recharging its batteries, and dreams are the soul's way of exploring all kinds of more or less "rational" experiences without the limits of the body. The soul doesn't know what rational means. That's why in a dream you can experience flying without any help, you can be in one place, only to be somewhere else the next second. The soul is unlimited in experiences, it is unlimited in time and space, and dreams are the place where it recalibrates itself to be able to sustain the effort of being temporarily confined in a body. This is also why babies start crying when they are born. Because their soul has entered a body that limits their experience of being and they need time to adjust to the new form. The physical state is an abnormal state. When you are in the spiritual state, that is your natural state. So, there is no such thing as someone leaving this life without the soul having chosen it, even death in a terrible accident or the death of a child.

WOMAN: But that's outrageous! You can't tell a mother who has just lost her child that the child's soul chose to die.

MONK: Let's get a couple things straight. First, nothing dies, everything transforms. Everything happens in cycles. From nature with its seasons to the financial world, everything happens in cycles. Life itself is a cycle — you are born, you grow, you reproduce, and you die. You come here to express, experience, integrate, and transcend. When you are young, you express yourself: you cry, you laugh, you imitate what you see around you. When you grow up, you experience yourself through feelings, through learning, through a job. When you reproduce, you integrate, and when you die, you transcend. Death is not bad, it's freedom! It is the Universe's gift to the soul. It is the gift of liberation from one's own creation, to be able to start again and again.

WOMAN: But what has the financial world got to do with it? You mentioned the financial world as a cycle.

MONK: I understand! Most people believe that the spiritual world and the financial world are completely separate things and should not be mixed, but it is precisely their separation that makes life even more difficult. The same applies to the separation between the spiritual world and everything that has to do with our sexual selves. The separation leads to everything sexual being considered taboo, even shameful. The fact that some think that spirituality means abstinence is so absurd. Why do you think God invented sex?

WOMAN: Because he was bored and didn't know what to invent in this relatively fabulous world we live in?

MONK: Great answer, but not really. Love means the deepest level connection. It means to experience oneness. Love done at the highest form, from the crown chakra, means to experience oneness, when before your eyes two become one — the same spirit united in the divine.

WOMAN: Crown chakra? I thought sexuality was root chakra.

MONK: I didn't say which chakra it belongs to, I said from which chakra it acts. Indeed, sex belongs to the root chakra, which is the basic biological level in procreation, but I meant the chakra from which one acts. When you act exclusively from the same chakra, the root chakra, sex is something strictly based on procreation, something animalistic. But acting from a higher chakra, the crown chakra, is a different experience. There, the air you breathe becomes the air the other breathes, your heartbeat becomes the other's heartbeat, everything synchronizes and you become one. This is the most sublime experience of oneness you can experience here.

WOMAN: Okay, I understand about sexuality, but what does the financial world have to do with spirituality? Corporations have nothing to do with spirituality, and spirituality has nothing to do with corporations. Money has nothing to do with spirituality, and spirituality has nothing to do with money.

MONK: It has all the connection in the world. Everything is interconnected. We started from the idea that everything happens in cycles, just like the seasons: we have winter and summer, death and birth. The same happens in the financial world. There are financial crises, followed by periods of economic prosperity, then financial crises again and then prosperity again. Not to mention the fact that when this marriage between finance and spirituality takes place, people feel that they are doing things with meaning. When they look back, they see that it really was worth it. The financial world is not actually separate from spirituality. Everything is interconnected. Does it seem strange to you that terms like fees, commissions, trading, dividends can be intertwined with acceptance, detachment, peace, and patience?

WOMAN: Somehow yes. Don't tell me that, besides being an engineer in this life, you were also an accountant!

MONK: Dear soul, poverty is not a virtue! Remember this. You are here to experience abundance in all its forms. The Bible of Christianity says that the poor will go to heaven, and you have chosen to believe this. Money is neither good nor bad. It is a form of energy. When you are obsessed with it and want to have it at any cost, it will run away from you. But when you are focused on bringing value, it will come to you on its own without you even realizing it. This happens because instead of chasing butterflies to catch them, you've created a garden where they come on their own.

WOMAN: So, can spiritual teachings be applied to the financial world?

MONK: Of course, you can apply them anywhere! As I said, daily activities cannot be separated from our spiritual evolution, because they are our very spiritual life! Two years ago, a young trader about your age came to me from London. He worked in the Forex market, which is quite a demanding field. He couldn't understand why he couldn't make the profits he wanted. He seemed to have no shortage of technical information, but nevertheless he felt stuck, so he left everything behind for a while to come here. Eventually, he learned the importance of accepting loss because he realized that he had a defensive attitude toward it. He couldn't accept losing. He was basically resisting loss, and we already know that when you resist anything, it persists. Then patience forms. He thought he had enough patience to get here.

WOMAN: Now I understand the interconnectedness of things, but really, we've been taught that money is the "root of all evil" or something unholy.

MONK: Not at all! It's neither good nor bad. It has a neutral value. Ultimately, all areas are related to spirituality, nothing is separate. Now I think we can come back to our subject of death, because we've digressed a bit. Of course, if other questions arise along the way, we can stop and discuss them.

Chapter 11

Karma and Rightful Mistakes

MONK: So, coming back, spirit and mind are immortal. They return to the astral, where they can choose their next adventure.

WOMAN: Is the mind immortal?

MONK: Exactly, I said spirit and mind, not heart and brain. We have the impression that the mind and the brain are the same thing, but the mind is not just in the brain, it envelops every cell in the body. For Buddhists, the brain is not the same as the mind, although in some ways the mind can be said to be located near the brain, where we have the third eye, also known as the pineal gland. So, our mind can reach as far as the ends of our hands or feet.

WOMAN: If the mind is in every cell of the body, then where is the spirit?

MONK: Spirit embraces the whole body and goes beyond. You can think of it as a kind of aura. Spirit owns the body, not the other way around. It is important to understand that we are a spirit holding a body and not a body holding a spirit. Spirit embraces the whole body and exists beyond it.

WOMAN: That's wonderful! Until now I thought that the spirit is inside the body and the mind is only in the brain, or they are somehow the same thing, although now I understand that the mind is a non-volatile form of memory that is never erased and records everything.

MONK: Exactly! It's a very good analogy. You can look at it this way.

WOMAN: Does that mean we can access experiences and see other past lives?

MONK: Of course! It is no longer a secret that little ones of 3 or 4 years old remember being pilots or soldiers and can recount in great detail, from names to specific events they could not possibly know about.

WOMAN: But how do you know that those events are not pure imagination?

MONK: Because those events have been checked in the archives and have been confirmed. You see, children especially have this power to remember past lives because they are closest to Source. This is why you can often see children who seem to be talking to themselves or to someone imaginary. They can communicate with the spiritual world most easily.

WOMAN: Yes, but this is labelled as abnormal and is considered a problem. It seems that the West is not ready for these things. The result? Most of these children are sent to psychologists for therapy. It's sad.

MONK: Indeed, most are not ready for these things, but you see, everyone is exactly where they should be. The question is not whether we will wake up, but when each of us will.

WOMAN: So how can we access our past lives? That sounds like an interesting topic.

MONK: It depends. You call it regressive hypnosis, which is conducted by a psychologist or a licensed professional, but you can also get yourself into that state where you access your past lives. In a deeply meditative state, you can even detach from your body and return to it. Thus, it is also possible to access your past lives. You can be led on this inner journey by your spiritual guides.

WOMAN: Spiritual guides? You mean angels?

MONK: You can call them whatever you want. Just as God can be called the Divine Intelligence, the Source, or the Universe, so you can call these guides whatever you like. In essence, whatever you call them, they are entities of light.

WOMAN: We call them angels. When I was little, my grandmother taught me "Guardian Angel." It's a beautiful prayer. I can still remember the words I used to say before bedtime, and I can remember her. She had such a kind soul. I often miss her, but I am sure that from wherever she is, she is watching over us and she is happy.

MONK: Absolutely! So, you can call your guide an angel or whatever you like. This entity, whatever you call it, is always by your side and can guide you if you ask and give it permission to do so. But without your consent, it cannot intervene, because it would violate your free will.

WOMAN: Hmm .... I think I'll talk to it more often. I often feel that someone is near me, like an unseen presence, but one that I can feel. By the way, about past lives, can I see how many I've had?

MONK: Of course, but what is important in this context? It's not how many lives you've had, it's the intensity with which you've lived them. You could have only ten lives lived deeply or hundreds that were not as memorable. A spirit's maturity is not determined by the number of lives lived, just as a person's age in this world does not automatically guarantee wisdom. You may have noticed children who are much wiser than their parents. Age is just a number and does not necessarily imply an increase in wisdom with it. The same perspective applies to the idea that some people, including children or teenagers, "leave too early." Apart from the fact that no one leaves this world without choosing to do so, it is not how many years you live in this life that matters, but how you live those years. You could live only 30 years and still have all the experiences you wanted to have in this life, or you could live 80 years and not have the courage to live authentically. So, as I said, death is not the worst of the options, but feeling like you haven't lived your *True Self* might be.

WOMAN: It's an interesting perspective to look at things. What can you tell me about people who commit suicide? Do they get the maximum punishment? In Christianity this is seen as a great sin.

MONK: As I said, nobody punishes anybody. There is no notion of "punishment" in the spirit world, much less the notion of "sin." The idea behind it is that by not facing the pain or the experience that led to the suicide, you'll have to come in another life to face the same problem.

WOMAN: I understand. It sounds nice, but I'm still not at peace with death, although at least conceptually I understand that one has many lives and that death is just an illusion.

MONK: I suggest we have a lesson in imagination. It'll do you good. Imagine you're already dead.

WOMAN: You mean what would I do if this was my last day?

MONK: No. Imagine that you are already dead and that your soul floats smoothly above your body. What would you do? What would you see? What would you have wanted to do before that moment?

WOMAN: I can't imagine such a thing! It seems far too painful. Why does death seem the only certainty we have in this life?

MONK: Because it's the only guarantee we have. Let's make it a joyous, celebratory moment! The water lily needs mud to bloom in all its splendour. Would you rather be a gardener in the middle of a war or a warrior in a garden? Let's prepare for that moment when we return to our spiritual family.

WOMAN: Oh, good! I float above my body and seem to feel so free and light. I see my family crying beside me because I'm no longer with them, but I'm with them, they just can't see me. I don't understand why they are crying because I am with them and I feel so light, just like a snowflake. I wish I could tell them I love them, even if they weren't the perfect family, because I realized too late how perfect they are. I wish I would have told them not to cry when I'm gone, but to rejoice because I am in the most wonderful place possible. It seems like nothing matters anymore, because really nothing matters anymore — not the little imperfections I was almost obsessed with, not what other people think, not the insignificant quarrels, not the distrust, the criticism. Everything dissipates. It is as if every particle of me has been cleansed and is full of light.

MONK: Great! You did very well. You remembered your true state of being!

WOMAN: I don't know where these words came from, but thank you! It's like something inside me knows how things will be after I'm gone. Sometimes I have a strange feeling of longing to go back home ... to my real home. I can't define that place. I just know it exists and it's so familiar. It's an overwhelming feeling that I don't belong in this world and I want to go back home.

MONK: But there's nothing strange. You have this feeling of not belonging because you really don't belong and we don't belong to this world. We're here to act in a movie. When the movie is over, we'll all go back home and choose other lives, other missions, other experiences.

WOMAN: In a way, death starts to not seem so monstrous, but how can you tell a mother who has just lost her child that the child has chosen this on a spiritual level? It's too much pain to comprehend, and seems absurd to most people anyway.

MONK: You see, if parents understood that they don't own their children, but are only guides for those souls, the separation from this world would be much easier. Each soul has its mission here on Earth, which may end sooner or later, and then each soul returns to the astral. If they knew what that place was like, they would be happy for those souls. To imagine what a soul feels like in the astral, think of children when they are young. They are closest to the astral world. Remember when you used to play with no sense of time? When you were playing without knowing what time it is, what day or month or year it is. Because in the astral there is no time. Remember when you were a little girl and you didn't know what fear was? Because all you were was love, light in all forms. Just breathing life. That's just a small piece of what a spirit is on the astral level. So why wouldn't you rejoice knowing that someone you love is getting there? You don't rejoice and you let the deep grief envelop you only when you don't know how things really are and you think that your loved one is gone forever, but this is not true. That is why, in some parts of the world, death is a celebration, because it really is a cause for joy, which some cultures have understood.

WOMAN: I've noticed this, people dress in white, like at weddings, instead of black.

MONK: Exactly! As I've said before, physical death is not the worst, although most people are terrified of it and act accordingly, bound by irrational fears and anxiety, all of which have as their cause the fear of death, of annihilation. Fear of death, that hidden, abiding fear that no amount of money or power can neutralize — that is the epicentre. If people knew that life is endless and that we never die, then fear would dissolve. How comforting it would be to people to know that they have lived countless times before and will live again! If they knew that guardian angels, guides really existed, people would feel much safer. From the fear of heights to the fear of public speaking, it all stems from the fear of death. You're not afraid of heights, you're afraid of falling, so you're afraid of death. You're not afraid of public speaking, but you're afraid of what others will think, implicitly you're afraid of exclusion, of annihilation.

WOMAN: But how can we make the death of a loved one not affect us so much?

MONK: Through awareness! I can't emphasize enough how important it is to know who you Truly are! When every cell in your body senses the Truth, there is no fear of death, there is no fear of anything, and you begin to truly live and enjoy this ephemeral experience on Earth. You see, when you look at the people in front of you only in terms of the body, the shell, and there is a huge attachment, the loss of a loved one will hit you in the most crushing way. Why? Because you experienced an attachment to that body and saw more the surface than what lies beyond it. Attachment is not love. When you know who you really are, then you know who others really are. Then you see straight through every body, beyond what is on the surface — you see the light and the expansion of the spirit. You see the greatness of the spirit beyond the illusion of masks, beyond ego, beyond pride, malice, vanity. Knowing that we are eternal, that we are forever, we free ourselves from the fear of death. We go through so many stages while we're here. We leave a baby's body, we pass into a child's body, then from child to adult, from adult to elder. Why don't we go a step further and leave the body of an elder and move to a spiritual plane? Ultimately, that's what we do. We never stop growing and evolving. Even when we reach the spiritual side, we continue to develop. In the depth of the soul, of the spirit, of the Source, where ideas are created, where there is only love, that's where it's worth going. Get rid of the fear. So much fear — fear of what others think, fear of dreaming, fear of hoping, fear of being judged. To come here and to discover that all the fears are just illusions is the greatest liberation you can experience.

WOMAN: Yes, but there can also be karmic fears from other lifetimes that we can't escape.

MONK: There is no such thing! The term "karma" has been taken over and misunderstood in the West, ascribing great weight to it. Indeed, there may be certain fears or traumas that migrate from a previous life, but that doesn't mean that we can't get rid of them or that they are permanent. Karma is simply a lesson that repeats until you understand its meaning. When you realize and integrate the teachings of that lesson, it will disappear. Karma is not a punishment. You receive what you have given in one form or another because you do not understand your true nature: that you are me, and I am you, and we are all one. When you hurt someone, it's like hurting yourself. When you steal from someone, it's like stealing from yourself. Therefore, the idea that God is punishing you is pure madness. He doesn't actually punish you. You punish yourself without even realizing you are doing it. Ultimately, karma is no more and no less than a lesson. If the spirit wishes to experience forgiveness and in a previous life did not have the opportunity or had it only partially, then it is possible to be faced in the present life with various situations, more or less intense, from which one may learn this lesson.

WOMAN: I understand, but since you mentioned forgiveness, why is it so important?

MONK: It is important because there is nothing to forgive.

WOMAN: What?

MONK: You heard me very well. There is nothing to forgive. Back to the meaning of life. The purpose of the Universe is that you live every possibility in every time and space. That's why in one life you are woman or man, victim or perpetrator, to experience every possibility, every reality from different angles. Ultimately, you came here to experience a scenario you wrote. In this scenario, you wrote about a woman who experiences betrayal, injustice, and in the aftermath experiences forgiveness. You wrote about an accident in which you almost lost your life, and you shared this script with several actors to help you stage this play. So, what is there to forgive? Nothing. Why not forgive yourself and others? It's like not forgiving yourself for acting in your own hand-written script, or not forgiving others for acting so well.

WOMAN: But life is not a movie script. It's real!

MONK: It only seems real. In a movie that you're watching where the actors are experiencing a powerful event, like a death or an intense kiss, you're experiencing those emotions. Physically, your body chemistry feels those emotions. Is that movie real? It's not, but for the two hours the movie lasts, you feel that it's real, that you are part of it. That's the whole point of life, that for a few hours or a few decades it feels real.

WOMAN: I understand and it makes sense, but sometimes it's very difficult to put into practice, especially to forgive those people who have hurt you so much.

MONK: I repeat, there is nothing to forgive! You wrote this script with your own hands. Better said, with your spirit, but you get the idea. The people who hurt the most are the ones most in need of love and forgiveness. They've chosen the hardest role to play. Before you came here, they asked you to remember to love and forgive them. Christianity provides a relevant scene here. Judas is perhaps the most hated man of all religions because he betrayed Jesus. While everyone blamed him, Jesus not only did not blame him, but was profoundly grateful that he loved him enough to take on the role of betrayer in order for him to fulfill his mission.

WOMAN: Are you saying that like Jesus we should forgive those who do us wrong, thinking that they are helping us to fulfill our own mission? From simple lies to betrayals and wars? Should we forgive all these colossal mistakes?

MONK: They are rightful mistakes. All mistakes are blessings. In every mistake, in every war, in every catastrophe there is a seed of change, a desire for liberation. In every suffering the rebellion, the desire to liberate, to grow, to break out of old patterns, structures, and connect to the soul is born. So, forgiveness is the key to liberation of the soul.

Chapter 12

Lao Tzu and the Ultimate Truth

WOMAN: You mentioned when we talked about physical death, that beyond it, at the astral level, we experience a unique state of wholeness. Can you describe that state in more detail?

MONK: Of course, but words cannot sufficiently describe that state. That genuine happiness cannot be compared to anything. It's as if time and space dissipate. Polarity disappears. All that remains is your ultimate state of being. Some people experience it right here, through meditation, prayer or other forms. It can even be expressed through dance, in a deep experience, or any other way.

WOMAN: I think I had such an experience in a dream. It was as if a bright white light was shining through every chakra, starting from the first chakra to the last. In the crown chakra, that blinding light exploded, and a luminous figure, whose face I couldn't see, whispered to me that I was free. In that moment I woke up and felt the greatest happiness, love and gratitude I have ever felt. When I looked at the clock, it was around five in the morning and the sun was about to rise. I started crying with happiness. I cannot express in words the happiness I felt. It was like a natural state of being. I can't compare it to anything else.

MONK: Hmm ... an expression of Kundalini. It's really wonderful. I told you we could celebrate. You chose to wake up.

WOMAN: Did I choose? I thought I was chosen.

MONK: No one is chosen by anyone. Choosing someone or something means that God or whatever you want to call him has preferences. Those who seem "chosen" are those who have chosen. Those who choose to look deep within, to see the structure of cells, atoms, to understand the dance of electrons, to perceive the light that creates matter, these are the ones who experience one of the most fascinating dimensions. To look deep inward instead of looking up to the heavens is the fifth dimension. This is the path that the great masters of history have followed. The fifth dimension means seeing coherence in everything. This is enlightenment. And we can also realize it here. So, enjoy this experience. It brings with it many other experiences.

WOMAN: That's right. Sometimes I happen to dream things that sooner or later happen in reality. Like when I dreamt of a plane almost landing, with no wings, and when I woke up, I found out that there had been a plane crash in Nepal on landing, with countless victims. Or I happen to dream about places I end up visiting at a later time. The funniest experience I had was when I dreamed that I was in a fall forest on a hill and, when I turned around, I saw a friend eating a red velvet cupcake. I forgot about that dream, but a few weeks later I ended up at a Japanese retreat that had a forest on a hill exactly like the one in my dream. I felt the same vibe as in the dream when I explored the place in more detail and, looking back, I spotted a Torii gate and a bridge painted exactly that deep red from the red velvet cake my friend was eating in the dream. It wasn't the cake, but I found and felt that deep red in that gate. What was interesting is that I didn't feel the vibration of that place when I first saw it. I only felt that vibration when I went far enough up through the woods, just like I did in the dream, and then I turned around and saw the red gate and bridge. It was as if that dream had come true before my eyes, like a lightning revelation.

MONK: Seeing into the future, spontaneous healing, are just some of the experiences that occur when you choose to see beyond the dimension we are in.

WOMAN: Why is this happening?

MONK: Let's see. Why do you think this is happening? Why do visions and miracles not take place in this dimension?

WOMAN: Could it be because of the different vibration between dimensions?

MONK: Exactly! Our third dimension has a much lower vibration than the fifth one. The third dimension is the dimension of matter. So, the faster you vibrate, the higher dimension you get to experience. You get to see electrons moving through time and space. In a higher dimension where the vibration is much faster, diseases begin to dissipate. There is no more health and disease, because there is no polarity. You may have heard of people who haven't had an illness or health problems for years. That's because regardless of their social or economic condition, their vibration is predominantly high.

WOMAN: Sounds wonderful. Isn't there a spaceship we can take to get out of here after we understand these things, this whole illusion? Now I think I can die in peace, knowing all these things.

MONK: "A man with outward courage dares to die. A man with inner courage dares to live" — these are perhaps some of Lao Tzu's most famous words.

WOMAN: Oh ... did you really answer everything?!

MONK: Those who come to experience the fifth dimension have the greatest responsibility, a much greater responsibility than the others. They help indirectly through their own awakening to awaken others, but also directly if they choose to do so. This is why there are masters all over the planet right now. Buddha, Jesus and others were not alone. The purpose of the Universe is evolution. In one way or another, every soul is evolving. So, it doesn't matter whether we talk about Jesus, Buddha, Mohammed, Christianity, Judaism, Buddhism or any other religion. They are all aspects of God, of the Source. All are connected through time and space by the same path to the core of ultimate truth. It is a path between self and Source, between you and God, expressed from different perspectives.

WOMAN: Then, if there are many paths to the ultimate truth, how can it be ultimate? It sounds like a contradiction.

MONK: This is the Divine Dichotomy — two or more truths can exist simultaneously in the same time and space. Let's simplify things. Imagine the Universe as a huge sphere, in the centre of which is the Source, the master template that connects every point in the sphere. It doesn't matter which path you choose to take to get to the middle, whether you choose to go left, right, up, down, straight to the middle, or to intersect with multiple perspectives of reality or none at all. These are all different aspects of the same reality. Let's take some examples. Let's say you are a point in the sphere, represented by the self. Your self is the sum of "I am." So, you can say, "I am from California. I am a patient person. I have brown hair." All this and what your self represents may or may not intersect with other realities. If they don't intersect, your path leads directly to the Source, God, the centre of the sphere. If they intersect with other realities, then your path will change direction, but you will still reach the Source, God, the centre of the sphere, at some point. For example, if you are now a brunette and you choose to dye your hair a different colour, or if you are now an impatient person and you choose to become a patient one, these are choices that change your path, but they will still lead you to the centre of the sphere. These are trivial examples, but I think you get the idea. You'll cross other paths, you'll make other choices, but you'll still get to the Source, to God, to the centre of the sphere. Now imagine that the sphere contains every self on this planet, every self on other planets, every object, plant, animal, phenomenon. That sphere contains everything. All these are expressions of God. Now do you understand the truth behind the idea that God is in all things? He expresses Himself through us all, through every way and reality, through every object. Therefore, He is Everything and Nothing. He is Alpha and Omega. So, there is no absolute truth, no universal right or wrong way. Christianity is no better than Judaism. The white race is not superior to the black race because each is an expression of divinity.

WOMAN: I would never have thought of seeing things this way, but I'm beginning to love it.

MONK: I'm glad to hear that. The same thing happens with a potato. It can be in different forms, like mashed potatoes, French fries, potato stew, but it's still a potato, it's just experiencing more perspectives, more ways of being. So, there is not just one way you can go. There is not just one truth that you have to follow. You just have to follow your own truth. That is why it is important to live by the *True Self*. Self is "So Hum" — I am one with all life and all life is one with me. The Universe exists in me as I exist in the Universe. That is why it is important to embrace every religion, every culture, every race, every history, every civilization, because none is against the other. None is better than the other. They all converge toward the same centre of reality — toward God.

WOMAN: So much wisdom in these words! What can you tell me about dharma and its meaning? About karma, you mentioned that it is just a lesson.

MONK: Of course, dharma is a karma from which the lesson has been learned. Also, dharma refers to the gifts that we have in this life that we have chosen. These may be talents, qualities or material possessions. Even your mission can become dharma. Therefore, when you don't follow your dharma, that is, you don't follow your dream, your body starts giving signals in many forms — persistent fatigue, frustration, or even an accident may occur.

WOMAN: What if I don't want to follow my dharma anymore?

MONK: That's the whole point. You want to follow it because you have chosen these gifts. Your soul yearns to follow your dharma and enjoy it. It can be a talent such as painting, writing, singing, gardening, the ability to help people in various forms, or anything else. The one who doesn't want to follow dharma may just be the mind. It comes up with arguments that seem sound and pertinent, to whom dharma seems childish, unrealistic. Most of the time, when you don't follow your dharma, you feel that you are not living according to the *True You*, the *True Self*. In other words, when you don't live your dream, it ends up hunting you.

WOMAN: I'm a little confused here. Some recommend making a public declaration in front of family or people close to us that we are committed to accomplishing something, a dream. On the other hand, others advise us to quietly work on our dream because outside energy can negatively influence it. What do you recommend?

MONK: I don't recommend anything. What works for you may not work for someone else. There is not just one way to get to your destination. So, choose what you feel is right for you. When your mind and soul choose one solution, it means that is the answer for you at that moment. You see, maybe revealing your plan or dream to someone else makes you feel like you make a commitment and can motivate you to fulfill it. At the same time, to someone else it may feel like an extra burden or additional pressure. What's more, if you follow the teachings of writing your dream with a pen and your path with a pencil, you will find it even harder to keep your promise to others, because you will often use erasers along the way. This can be seen as "paralysis" from the outside, but it's just redirection, often to a much better path.

WOMAN: Then why is it that sometimes dharma seems to have so many hindrances and is more like karma?

MONK: Dharma has no hindrances. The only one that comes up with contradictory arguments is the mind. For example, if your dharma is to write, then your mind can come up with dozens, hundreds of counterarguments — "I'm not good enough," "who do you think you are to write," "you can't make a living from writing," "my teachers didn't encourage me to do it," and so on. Then what is known as "artistic block" can occur, because you disconnect from the Source and live your life in fear, listening to your mind or to others who "are right." Understand that the mind is not an ineffective tool, but we need to know how to interact with it. It is therefore important to bring both mind and soul on the same path.

WOMAN: But how?

MONK: Don't disconnect from the Source! Let the Universe deal with the "how," and you just answer the "why." The "why" question, as far as the dharma is concerned, is easy to answer, because it is hard to give an answer.

WOMAN: What?

MONK: You can't give a concrete answer to "why" you like writing or gardening. You simply answer that you like it because you enjoy it, because you feel like doing it. And that's all we need. The next step to move forward is to take the mind aside, just like talking to a child. We explain to it that it is safe, that it has nothing to worry about if we choose this path, that we understand its worries, its fear of the unknown.

Chapter 13

Manifestation: "Hoping" or "Knowing"

WOMAN: I really wish to become like you, to have your wisdom.

MONK: I am truly flattered to hear those words.

WOMAN: But, honestly, how did you manage to acquire this wisdom?

MONK: I think we've still got a vacancy here for you for the next three decades.

WOMAN: Hey, I'm serious! How did you do it?

MONK: Surrender into nothing to become everything.

WOMAN: What? Sounds confusing.

MONK: Exactly! Surrender into nothing to become everything or surrender into darkness to become light. Have you noticed that stars shine brightest and show their beauty in an environment where there is no light pollution? In the mountains or away from cities.

WOMAN: Of course. That's why every year we go to see shooting stars in an area outside the city. In the city you can hardly see them.

MONK: That's exactly the case of wisdom. It shines brightest in darkness. In darkness, in nothingness, you become light, you become everything. Yes, this is not easy in many ways. First of all, most people tend to be obsessively in control of life, and surrender is not about control or resistance. Surrender in anything means faith, it means letting go of control, it means clearing out all or at least most of our mental patterns, it means being in the flow of life. Ultimately, it means letting go of falling, knowing that God, the Source, the Universe, or whatever you want to call it, will catch you in its arms.

WOMAN: I think a lot of people are afraid they're going to fall and break their neck.

MONK: Exactly! And so, the magic is broken. They even fall, not realizing that the magic is broken precisely because of them. They are taken over by a moment of fear that extinguished the flame of magic — fear, which is not faith. In other words, they had no faith, the faith that means realizing who you really are. A vicious circle, no?

WOMAN: Then what would be the first step to wisdom?

MONK: Find out, remember what you truly are! Not Mary from Los Angeles, California. Not Kara from Munich, Germany. Not Ming from Beijing, China. Find out who you really are!

WOMAN: A soul who came to experience the relative, love, stardust, part of divinity, divinity itself — one and at the same time all. Each soul is a divine spark, having multiple experiences to return to the unique consciousness. We are all interconnected, each one of us an expression of the divine, experiencing life in different forms and ways.

MONK: Wonderful! Now that you know what you are on a declarative level, experience, feel these things to the core, absorb them like a sponge into your whole being! Believe in who you are, like children believe in Santa Claus. Believe in who you are, like you did with the healing you told me about. Remember? The one in which you believed during your healing through every pore while doctors gave you no diagnosis for your problem. The one where you changed the chemistry of your cells and gave them vitality and health by faith. That's the faith we're talking about. It's not enough to know declaratively what the power of high, elevated emotions is. They deserve to be assimilated by the body, like a medicine that is swallowed and spreads throughout the body. Of course, the declarative level, where you know these things, is the first step. The next is assimilating them at the subconscious level, at the level of every cell in the body. So, we begin to transform our inner vibration.

WOMAN: But how do we get our vibration higher?

MONK: Back to what I said about the frequency of emotions. If water can turn into steam or ice, then steam and ice can turn into water. Steam, ice, and water are the same thing, vibrating at a different frequency. Matter can become energy and energy can become matter. This is science. Remember Einstein's well-known formula, $E = mc^2$? "E" is energy, "m" is mass, and "c" is the speed of light. Thoughts are waves. Waves carry frequencies and energy. Mass also carries frequency and energy. Mass is related to time and space. Waves exist everywhere, beyond time and space. If you can imagine your desire, then it already exists in another dimension, in the quantum field, it just doesn't have mass yet. All waves exist in the quantum field. What you seek is already seeking you.

WOMAN: So many scientific details .... I feel like I'm talking to a scientist, not to a spiritual person.

MONK: I have already told you that science does not exclude spirituality, and spirituality does not exclude science. In the financial world, money does not exclude spirituality, and spirituality does not exclude the financial world. Nothing is separate!

WOMAN: I understand. Just teasing! I always thought that the masters, Tibetan monks and all the wise minds in the East always have those serious faces, but here I was surprised! People often mistake seriousness for sadness or sternness on faces. They think that if you smile or laugh, you are not serious enough.

MONK: Indeed! We need people who smile more often.

WOMAN: So, going back to "our science," are you saying that our emotions are the light in Einstein's equation? Then I understand that quantum field levels are just different realities, and our mind can choose that frequency. Since thoughts are waves, they determine the reality we live in. We give thoughts energy through emotions. Emotions are energy in motion. So, we can make a quantum leap into the desired reality.

MONK: Exactly! Everything is energy. Everything vibrates. I cannot emphasize these things enough. Remember that emotion is the fuel of the body. It is energy in motion. Knowing this, we move on, because emotions are divided into creative and stagnant or constructive and destructive emotions. Love has one of the highest vibrations. Therefore, the longer you stay in high and expansive vibrations, the faster you get to materialize desires. Everything begins to happen effortlessly. Synchronicities, opportunities begin to appear out of nowhere. You become a magnet that attracts what it is. You already know we get what we are, not what we want. So, peace, joy, love, acceptance, excitement, optimism are some of the elevated emotions most worth spending time on. On the other hand, emotions like fear, hatred, shame, guilt, worry, anger are not only non-elevated and attract an unpleasant and unwanted reality, but they are also energy consuming. You can't see your reflection in boiling water, right? In exactly the same way, you can't see the truth in a state of anger. When the water is calm, clarity emerges. You know they say boats don't sink because there's water around them. They sink because water gets inside them. You don't become bad because there is badness around you. You become bad because you let the badness come inside you.

WOMAN: So, it's important to stay in high, elevated emotions.

MONK: Exactly! And as I said, these emotions cannot be rationalized. They have to be felt, they have to be part of you. I know I often use this "must," but remember that nothing is obligatory. All these things, which seem more or less crazy to the rational, are *worth* it. They are not a "must." Remember the sponge analogy. These emotions deserve to be absorbed by every cell, every atom, every quark in the body. That's why most people in manifestation who try superficial gratitude, made out of the rational, see that it doesn't work in two days and give up. Gratitude, especially when you have lived a life in ingratitude, is a process that takes time, because there are three stages of gratitude that are good to know. The first stage is when you first learn about the power of gratitude and find all the reasons to ignore it — "I don't have the relationship I want," "I don't have millions of dollars in my bank account," "I don't have a fancy car in the garage." In this phase you find all the reasons why you shouldn't feel grateful. The second stage of gratitude, if you choose to go further, is rationalized gratitude. Here begins a rational process in which the mind searches for reasons to be grateful — "I'm grateful for last week's pay raise," "I'm grateful for this new car." This is usually where the mind looks for those "big" things that stand out. Beyond that, the third stage is gratitude we feel. This is the most powerful and, once practiced, it begins to become a state of being. While rationalized gratitude looks for grandiose, big things from its perspective, felt gratitude looks more for seemingly small things — "I am so grateful for the chamomile flavoured tea in my cup," "I am so grateful for the warm sunlight touching my skin," "I am so grateful that I can feel the sand of the beach between my toes." These are not just on a mental level, they are felt and not just with the heart but with every cell in the body. This kind of gratitude is felt all the way down to the tips of the fingers and toes, in every part of the body. You see, mind, thought is just the machine you are in. To get moving, you need soul, emotion, otherwise the car won't start. It doesn't matter if you have the most grandiose car, the most grandiose thought, the car won't start without fuel, without emotion. I think it's much clearer now.

WOMAN: Of course. Somehow so simply put and yet so profound. We tend to complicate things, we tend to devise complex systems, we tend to think that anything complicated will lead to success and anything easy means failure. Too often we say to ourselves: "It's too simple. It can't be that easy!"

MONK: Indeed, these patterns are deeply ingrained in the subconscious, but remember that love is simple, gratitude is simple, happiness is simple. They are simplicity and grace. Finally, applied understanding is much deeper than information. Most people just know, but there are few who understand, who see beyond the senses, who integrate things. That's what manifestation is — the belief that whatever you want is already fulfilled. It is not an energy in which you "*hope*," it is an energy in which you *know* that something is already fulfilled.

WOMAN: But it's like lying to myself. How can I have an energy where I know that everything I want is already accomplished, when I'm living the reality where I don't see that thing?

MONK: The energy in which you know is not denying the reality of the present or rushing to get into that energy. The energy in which you know means acceptance of the present moment and total belief in the Universe, namely that that something is already fulfilled, a belief that requires patience. If there is no patience, there is no faith. All Christian, Muslim, Jewish prayers end with "Amen." Coming from Hebrew, this word means "so be it," or "true." It is a kind of seal which tells us that the prayer has already been fulfilled, it is in God's hands, in the hands of the Universe. It already exists. Remember the

CD analogy. If the tune is at minute 1:11, then minute 2:22 will not represent the future, because the tune is totally there presently. It already exists. It's the same with your desire. It already exists. You just have to be in its energy. Imagine that absolutely, like really absolutely everything you desire, every version of you already exists — the evil, judgmental, hateful, resentful version, the revenge-seeking version, the compassionate, wise version, the version of you with a pool house. Absolutely every version you can imagine, and even those you cannot, already exist.

WOMAN: My version with a luxury car in the garage? :)

MONK: Whatever version of you that you are and have already exists! You just have to choose it.

WOMAN: But how do I choose?

MONK: With the frequency you emit. Your frequency is currency in the vast catalogue of the Universe. The Universe says, *"Here: this is the infinite catalogue from which you can choose absolutely anything you want. The currency is your frequency."* You see, when your mind, your soul, and every cell in your body is aligned in frequency with what you want to choose from the vast catalogue of the Universe, that something will appear in your reality.

WOMAN: Even things that seem impossible?

MONK: You said it yourself — "things that seem impossible." They just seem. Nothing is impossible. Something was impossible until someone decided it was possible. It was a conscious choice of possibility, and then it became reality. You see, if you consider something to be impossible, then you will see the reality of that choice — the nothingness of impossibility ... until someone else decides to turn that impossible into possible. The same thing happens when you want something to "not" happen — "I don't want to be cheated," "I don't want to lose money." What will happen is that you will attract exactly those things into your life — you will get cheated and you will lose.

WOMAN: Is that because the Universe doesn't know what negation means, what "no" means?

MONK: It's not about that. You don't think the Universe is so dumb that it doesn't know what negation means. Let's analyse this a little bit. What is the energy behind denial, behind "no"? What do you feel when you say you don't want something to happen to you? Fear, right? There's so much fear behind that "no" that you're going to get exactly those things that you fear. You'll get exactly the things you're complaining about.

WOMAN: Hmm ... then "I don't want to be happy," "I don't want to have a fulfilled life," "I don't want to be rich".... Why are you laughing? It should work, to have a fulfilled and happy life.

MONK: As I said ... it's always a pleasure to meet Westerners in search of the meaning of life who are trying to fool the Universe. Ultimately, they're not fooling the Universe, they're fooling themselves. Do you feel fear when you say those things, when you say you're afraid to have a fulfilled life? I have said and I will say it again and again as often as necessary — emotion is the energy that embodies desire. Emotion, the sustained feeling, is what turns desire into reality. Why do I say sustained emotion? Because when emotion is not sustained it means that doubt is taking its place next to faith, and this is one of the greatest impediments to manifestation. Let's take an example. Let's say you want a new home for your family. The emotion around this wish is a strong one, because you love your family and want the best for them. Imagine this wish as a ball, and it is the emotion that will propel it into the arms of the Universe. Let's say for two weeks this emotion will persist and the Universe will receive this ball. But something happens. You start to think and feel that it's going to be hard, because the house payments are going to be high and it's going to be a huge strain on the family, or that at some point you're not going to have an income to pay those payments and you're going to lose the house. At this point it's like your ball hitting a wall. Depending on how long you sustain these emotions of fear, you will see one reality or another — either you will enjoy your new home with your family or this will be the biggest disappointment. Let's take another example. Let's say you're in a relationship with your new partner and things are going really well for the first few months — you feel love, understanding, and support. Then you feel something is happening. It all seems too good to be true and you start to feel and think that this scenario won't last, that your trust will be betrayed, that your partner will find someone else. Again, depending on which emotion you feed, that of love or that of fear, you will see your emotion expressed in reality. Now do you understand what it means and what is the power of a sustained emotion? It's up to you how much you support the emotion of love or fear. If you support the emotion of love more, then you will see a reality expressed as love, understanding, compassion. If you support the emotion of fear more, then you will see a reality expressed in the form of endless arguments. If you support both emotions equally, then you will see in your reality a confusion between the two realities, perhaps a relationship full of quarrels and reconciliations. This is why most consider the power of manifestation to be silly, because it doesn't sufficiently support that emotion, whose reality they want to see. In the end, manifestation works both ways. Therefore, feeling, emotion is a language that directs and focuses our consciousness. It is a state of being that we are in, rather than something we do at a particular time of day. Situated between science and ancient teachings, we know that creating reality is more than "*doing*" — it is "*being*." We must become the things we choose to experience. Lots of people want fulfilling relationships, where their ideal partner looks like this, is like this, does this, behaves like this, but do you know what makes that materialize into your reality?

WOMAN: Visualization? A list of what you want and you visualize it?

MONK: Make a list of all the qualities you want in your partner and become that list, no matter what kind of relationship we're talking about, friendship or love. You will get the reflection of who you are. Remember that everything begins and ends with you!

WOMAN: We should probably all remember this.

Chapter 14

You Are the Answer

WOMAN: Can we talk about the power of meditation and what it means?

MONK: Of course! What do you want to know about it?

WOMAN: What exactly happens when you are in that lotus position and meditating? You seem very focused.

MONK: We speak the language of the Universe — feeling and emotion.

WOMAN: What?

MONK: Just as you heard. Feeling, emotion is a language that has no external words or expressions. Our feelings and emotions are what affect the matter from which our reality is made. Emotion is energy. Science and spirituality already talk about this over and over again. The purpose of meditation is to quiet the mind and let the soul speak.

WOMAN: What kind of meditation do you recommend?

MONK: I have no recommendation. Just experiment with what suits you best. You may find it harder at first to get into that state where you quiet your mind, so you might want to try guided meditation. Or maybe you'll find yourself more in unguided meditation. Don't forget, too, that being in nature, where the sound of streams meets the rustle of tree leaves and birdsong, is also meditation. Strolling on the ocean or sea beach is also meditation.

WOMAN: I think I need a quiet room where I can meditate. Meditation will probably help me get my life in order.

MONK: The room is inside you.

WOMAN: But how can I meditate when all the thoughts come into my mind and there's an internal noise?

MONK: Just watch the thoughts come and go one after another. The heart always knows the answer. The challenge is to quiet the mind. Be the observer of your own thoughts. Here's a trick that will help you quiet your mind. Just ask yourself, "What is the source of the next thought?" In that moment, for a few moments, your thoughts will stop. Your attention will focus on the gap between thoughts. You can try other questions: "What is the colour or shape of the next thought?" It's not the question that's important, it's the attention you give to it. Close your eyes for a moment and just notice the thoughts coming and going, coming and going, one after another. Don't try to stop them. Don't judge them. Just observe them. Now ask yourself, "What is the source of the next thought?"

WOMAN: I can't believe it! I never thought it could be so simple to stop your thoughts. I tried all sorts of techniques, but none seemed to work.

MONK: Congratulations! You have just discovered pure consciousness. You wouldn't have known its experience if you didn't lack the experience. This void between thoughts has just helped you to experience it. Just remember: to experience and understand light, you have to experience darkness. Everything you know about light is because of the darkness. So, keep this state of awareness as long as possible. When you notice that thoughts start arising again, ask yourself the question once more to create the void. Over time, this practice will make it easier and easier to expand this awareness. You can also ask your heart anything. It always knows the answer.

WOMAN: But I tried to ask my heart. I got no answer. I always thought "ask your heart" was more of a nice metaphor than anything else.

MONK: We think of the heart in a poetic sense, the place of love and compassion, but it is more than that. The power of the heart is to connect with who you are in the deepest way. Some of the greatest questions asked of the heart unfold as a path, not as an answer. On the other hand, some answers appear "out of nowhere" from people's words, from a flyer dropped on the floor, from a newspaper headline, from a journey. The Universe always speaks to us — through dreams, numbers, animals, even people. You just have to be open to see and hear these answers. Perhaps the most important virtue is to see and hear beyond the senses, beyond the eyes and ears. To hear and see with the soul is the sublime experience everyone has access to. The answer is always within you. You are the answer. The answer is never outside you.

WOMAN: Sometimes I wish I could grasp the whole Universe with my mind, with its wisdom.

MONK: You don't have to. In fact, you can't do it. The Universe cannot be understood if you strive to do so. It can be understood if you don't try. You see, the Universe is vaster than thought and more limitless than imagination. To understand the Universe, look within and you will realize that you are the Universe itself. Your eyes, your iris, comprise whole galaxies. Your fingerprints are in the tree rings.

In your veins, if you look at your wrist, you will see the lightning in the sky, you will see the veins of leaves. In every organ of your body you will see fruits and vegetables. Our brain has the shape of a walnut kernel, our kidneys have the shape of beans, our heart has the shape of a tomato. In your hairs you'll find the blades of grass scattered on the fields. In the wrinkles of your fingers you will see mountains. In the cracks of your hands you will see the cracks of the earth. You are not just a fragment of the Universe. You are the Universe! You are one with the Universe, as the whole Universe is one with you. Therefore, to understand the Universe, it is enough to know yourself. Let me tell you a story about this. It is said that once upon a time, at the edge of a mountain village, a young shepherd was shepherding his flock of sheep from morning until night. At one point, he learned of a treasure hidden somewhere in the world and decided to leave everything to go and find it. He wandered for years over sea and land, desert and plain, but found nothing. Disappointed by his failure, he returned home, where the other shepherds needed him to dig a well. After three days of digging the well, something totally unexpected happened. The young shepherd stumbled upon a huge treasure of gems, each one brighter than the next. The moral? You see, sometimes we look so far outside ourselves for the answers when they're so close inside us. That's why, to understand the Universe, you only need to know yourself.

WOMAN: Nicely said, but sometimes I think excessively about all sorts of things and I don't know how to get rid of it. I feel it consumes so much of my energy unnecessarily.

MONK: Let's see. Overthinking about the future is because we make up stories about "how" things are supposed to happen as we try to control the future through every detail. We do this by trying our hardest, by any means necessary, to answer the question "how." Try to answer only the "why." That is the only question that really matters. Let the Universe deal with the how. This doesn't mean that you lie in bed all day thinking about the "why" with absolutely no action. It is true, if we were to speak in percentages, about 80% of what happens around us is based on who we are and only 20%, a tiny fraction, on what we do. But let's not forget that we are in a three-dimensional Universe that needs action on our part. Ultimately, what is magical is that even that 20% will be driven by who you are. The more you are open and leave the control for the "how" in the hands of the Universe, the more you will notice how things start to happen naturally, effortlessly, easily, and gracefully.

WOMAN: It's hard to give up control when you've heard all your life that "you have to work hard to have things."

MONK: If things were achieved through hard work, then why don't those who work all day, even overtime, in their offices get what they want? Because the major results in your life are a result of who you are, the energy you express, not what you do. Of course, hard work is also an option. It leads to raw manifestation, as I like to call it. It will bring you the result you want, but it will require hard work, fatigue, a lot of frustration, and sleepless nights. On the other hand, another option is natural manifestation, because it is already in your natural state of being. You are a co-creator, a manifestor. You are the artwork and, at the same time, you are the artist. While raw manifestation is based more on doing and less on being, natural manifestation is based more on being and less on doing. In natural manifestation, things happen with ease and grace.

WOMAN: So, if I understand correctly, the more I am in a felt state of gratitude, love, joy, the more I attract into my reality the life I want.

MONK: Exactly, dear soul! But coming back to your question about overthinking, I said that for forward thinking it is helpful to let go of control of the "how," to stop controlling every little detail, every movement. On the other hand, for thinking in the past, it is helpful to understand and integrate the fact that "everything is exactly as it should be," because most of the time excessive thinking in the past is rooted in regrets or "what ifs."

WOMAN: I understand. What can you tell me about expectations? I used to have and I still have times when I have expectations of others. The problem with them is that when they are not fulfilled, they cause a lot of pain and disappointment.

MONK: It's simple. Stop expecting!

WOMAN: Thank you! Very profound. How did I not think of that?!

MONK: Having expectations means wanting to control how a person should behave. Control means rigidity, and the Universe will teach you, one way or another, to give it up. Life happens in unexpected ways. Keep the dream, the desire alive, but allow the Universe to help you, because there is no one way to reach your destination. That's why they say write your dream with a pen and the path with a pencil. The Universe has ways you wouldn't even think of to help you reach your destination. So, let control go. Let me tell you another revealing story in this regard. There was a severe thunderstorm during which an entire village was flooded. All the people were climbing onto the roofs of their houses to survive. Rescuers arrived and rescued all the people except one who refused to leave. He hoped that God would save him, having been devoted to God all his life and obeying all His commands. Despite the rescuer's insistence, he vehemently refused to leave. The waters continued to rise, and eventually the roof was swallowed up and the man died. Arriving in heaven, angry and outraged at not being rescued, he complained to God: "All my life I have been devoted to you and have obeyed every commandment and word coming from you. Why have you not saved me?" God replied: "But I sent saviours to come and save you. Why didn't you get into the boat?" You see, sometimes we get stuck in our expectations without being open to all the opportunities that life brings, and then we get angry at God or the Universe for not helping us.

WOMAN: Indeed, it pays to be open to life even if, more often than not, the mind tells us that there are no opportunities in a particular direction. Perhaps, this closure to life is also because God has not been understood.

Chapter 15

The Bamboo Story

MONK: Indeed, God has not been understood. For centuries and millennia, religion has been distorted in countless ways. How do you think God's name, which is associated with love, peace and compassion, can be invoked to justify wars, murder and genocide? "Holiness" has infected the planet like a morbid disease, like a plague that has taken root everywhere. Too many people are more ritual-oriented and religious than spiritual. Wars, dirty business, good deeds are hidden behind so-called "holy beliefs." How can you kill in the name of faith? We kill each other because we believe that we are "different," that our ideology, our religion, is the "true" one. We forget that God is peace, that God is love, that there is only one religion — the religion of absolute love. Love is the way home. It is the only lesson we have to remember. If not, we will repeat again and again this grade called life, just like pupils failing at school.

WOMAN: I understand what you mean, but, you see, there are so many differences between us that not everyone can accept and consider them as threats, if not at least anomalies.

MONK: What differences? That someone is of one religion and someone is of another religion? That someone has one opinion and someone else has another opinion? That someone has chosen to have a marriage other than the "normal" one? Buddha was not a Buddhist. Jesus was not a Christian. Mohammed was not a Muslim. We're all in the same boat. What you call differences are just superficial and unimportant things. We look so much at the differences when the similarities are so overwhelming. If you look into the depths of every religion and every ritual, you will find amazing similarities. They all speak of love, forgiveness, kindness. We have killed each other in the name of religion, we have kept the hatred and resentment of centuries to bring back again and again to the present, reasons for pointless and impertinent wars. And this is because we have forgotten who we are. I have repeated and will repeat as often as necessary the importance of knowing who we really are. When you know and become aware that we are one, then the veil of forgetfulness begins to go down and you realize the majesty and beauty of life. We are love. You become a spiritual billionaire when your love is unconditional and absolute. Remember who you truly are and listen to the gentle whispers of your beautiful soul. Don't let your fears master the soft voice of intuition. We are eternal, immortal spirits. We are infinite love united in the divine.

WOMAN: Infinite love united in the divine. How sublime!

MONK: We have been taught that this is the only life we have. If you do good, you go to heaven, and if you do bad, you go to hell. That's how duality was born, which is considered evil. Somebody told us that the only way is light, that darkness is evil and must be denied, except that it is not spiritual, it is only biological. We considered sun, day, light to be something good, because it meant survival when wild animals were attacking — you could see them, and at night ... darkness was considered something bad, because animals were killing us and somebody could attack us. So light was good and darkness was bad because we could see and we could defend ourselves. In this way, a pattern was created throughout history, that darkness is bad and light is good. This is how the idea of heaven and hell was created — heaven with lots of light and hell with lots of darkness. When we did that, we separated the Universe into two and said that one of these two must be evil and the other good. Then it was said that we must transcend to the light and deny the darkness. Thus, millions of stories and legends were born in which a "hero," someone good, must fight the enemy, someone evil.

WOMAN: I can't believe it! This is madness! Do you realize that most religions base their theories on this duality of heaven and hell?

MONK: Insanity? Angels and demons work together. We have divided their work as if they were enemies, but they are not. They are friends and they help each other. We honour the darkness. In a higher Universe there is no duality. Only we in this dimension consider that. Honour the contrasts. With their help, you have discovered the brilliance of light.

WOMAN: What?

MONK: As I said, there is no right or wrong. Darkness and light are just tools to understand what we are.

WOMAN: Sometimes I'm afraid to find out more.

MONK: Fear is a waste of energy. It is a surface disturbance. It keeps you from accomplishing what you were sent to accomplish.

WOMAN: Sent to accomplish? I thought we had free will, that we had the power to choose. Then free will is a lie. How can I choose if my life has already been mapped out?

MONK: You've already made your choice. You are here to find out why you have chosen. You didn't come here to choose, you already have. Why would free will be a lie? You chose and wrote your script before you came here.

WOMAN: But does that mean I can't change it?

MONK: Of course, it can change if the soul feels so. You deserve the highest good.

WOMAN: Since you mentioned "deserve," have you ever considered that you don't deserve to have good things happen to you in life? I often come up against this belief.

MONK: You are not alone! Too many people judge and blame themselves, believing that they don't deserve to be happy, that they don't deserve for good things to happen to them. These are just deeply ingrained beliefs that you "have" to do something to deserve it, beliefs that are also reflected in the holy books. So many passages and verses that say that you "must" glorify Him, worship God in order to enter the Kingdom of Heaven, in order to deserve to receive good things. You don't have to do anything to deserve to be happy, to deserve to have good things happen to you! Too many people whip themselves, considering themselves sinners, unworthy, living in an energy of guilt and resentment. Remember that God does not judge you, does not punish you. You are the only one who does. Pause for a few moments, put your hands around your heart, say your name followed by "I love you" — "Carol, I love you!" Try it.

WOMAN: I've never done that. It sounds strange to say it to myself.

MONK: Everything has a beginning. It's okay to cry. Let the tears flow.

WOMAN: But ... why? I don't understand. Why do I feel this confusion of feelings?

MONK: How often do we say we love ourselves? We wait for others to say they love us, but do we love ourselves? Have we ever told ourselves how much we love ourselves? How can we expect someone else to tell us and show us love when we haven't said it to ourselves once in our lives? Or maybe you want to wait for science to prove these things — the power of love, compassion, gratitude.

WOMAN: I don't know what to say about science. They make some theories that later turn out to be untrue.

MONK: Science is a wonderful tool that has both its advantages and its disadvantages. It makes progress proving things, but it's really lagging behind at the moment. Science only discovered in the 20th century the existence of an energy field that interconnects everything. This was already known by ancient civilizations since the beginning of time. We often mistake technological advancement for evolution. Yes, ancient civilizations didn't have microwaves to heat food and telephones to communicate. Does that mean they weren't advanced? If communication was accomplished telepathically and food was instantly heated by the power of clear intent, then did they really need external, so-called "advanced" objects? Obviously not. So, the question of our technological evolution becomes a paradox — is this "evolution" really a sign of progress or regression?

WOMAN: We'll probably have to be patient to find out. What can you tell me about patience? Is it a virtue?

MONK: Patience, along with simplicity and compassion, is perhaps the most important virtue. Patience. Patience means caring with love and waiting with trust. Lack of patience leads to despair. The great teacher Lao Tzu himself said that he had only three things to teach —simplicity, patience, compassion. These three are your greatest treasures — simple in action and thought, you go back to the source of being; patient with both friends and enemies, you agree with the way things are; you are compassionate toward yourself, you reconcile all beings in the world.

WOMAN: But why is patience so important?

MONK: Because not having patience is not having trust. Patience is proof that you trust the Universe and who you really are. Let me tell you the story of the bamboo. It is said that on the outskirts of a village in China, there was a young man disillusioned by life's failures. Though he worked hard from morning until night, he always faced failure. At the end of his strength, he decided to set out into the world, not knowing which way to turn. One day he arrived at the edge of a forest where he met a wise monk who was admiring the beauty and greenery of the forest. "Isn't it wonderful to be surrounded by such beauty?" asked the monk. "It probably is" replied the young man thoughtfully. Seeing him so distressed, the monk asked him what brought him to those parts. The young man told the monk of all his failures and asked, "Why do I work from morning until night and see nothing?" Seeing the young man exhausted, the monk told him the story of the wisdom of the bamboo. "See those two plants over there? The fern and the bamboo?" asked the monk. "Of course," replied the young man, nodding affirmatively. Then the monk said: "I planted the seeds of the two plants together. I took proper care of both plants. I gave them food, water, sunlight and fertilizer, but the fern grew quickly in a short period, while the bamboo did not grow." Confused, the young man asked the monk why this was happening. The monk continued, "I took care of the bamboo for four years, but nothing happened. It didn't show the slightest sign of growth. But I didn't give up and continued to look after it. In the fifth year, the bamboo grew almost ninety meters tall in two months." Hearing this, the young man was amazed. He asked the monk: "How is such a thing possible?" The monk laughed and explained to the man that the little bamboo tree was using all its food to grow underground and develop a strong root system that would allow it to grow enormously tall. The bamboo had developed a strong foundation to help support itself for the years to come. The monk then asked the young man, "Do you understand now why all these failures? Why you seem to see nothing, though you work from morning until night?" "All my struggles are building my foundation for a better life," the young man replied, grateful to the monk for his wise words.

WOMAN: Interesting story. It reminded me of the famous words from Kybalion, *"As above, so below; as below, so above."* It's a great analogy with the bamboo story.

MONK: Axis mundi or world tree. It represents the connection between heaven and earth, between above and below. In almost every religion you will find interpretations of it. In Buddhism, you'll see it represented by the chakra system. Christianity and Islam also have their interpretations. All these interpretations ultimately talk about the principle of correspondence.

WOMAN: We should probably listen more to our inner voice, not because we "have to," but because it's worth it. Ultimately, everything we need is inside ourselves. We don't live on Earth. We are the Earth.

MONK: I'm glad to hear those words. You are beginning to understand things. At the same time, it seems that our talk is drawing to a close, dear soul. I'm sure you've found the answers to the questions that have been haunting you. Why are you crying?

WOMAN: Because ... it's like I've been living a lie until now, an illusion. So much unnecessary suffering. It's like a part of me has died, the old me has died, with all the ideas and preconceptions.

MONK: But you really died. You died and you were reborn. To come here and die and rediscover that death doesn't exist is the sublime experience. You feel that you lived in the lie because, in a way, you lived in it. By being disconnected from the Source, from the *True You*, you are living the biggest lie. But awakening is a feeling that cannot be described by this limited language of words. It is love, it is freedom, it is life rippling through every cell in your body. You are love! Let the child in you experience the beauty of life. Remember that you came to Earth on holiday.

WOMAN: I feel so free after finding out so many things, and at the same time I feel somehow betrayed that I found out these things so late.

MONK: Whatever you feel is perfectly normal. Don't deny what you feel. Don't judge. Just notice every thought, every emotion that comes and goes. You are neither your thoughts nor your emotions. You're just here to experience them. That's what makes the Earth experience really special.

WOMAN: Thank you! I have no words to express all the gratitude. I never would have thought that my life would change so much after such a talk. Do you think we can summarize the most important lessons from this conversation?

MONK: Well, I think we can group them into a few teachings:

1. Discover who you really are beyond any ideology, label, name, or nationality and integrate who you are into every pore of your skin. That is why you are here.

2. Believe everything and nothing. Pass everything through the filter of the *True Self*. Be curious like a small child experiencing life.

3. Believe with every cell in your body and sustain that belief. Remember the analogy of the sponge soaked in water. Feel faith through every pore of your skin. Be in an energy where you *know* that that something, whatever it is, is already fulfilled.

4. We are one and, at the same time, we are many. We are many and yet we are one. Celebrate both unity and individuality. Remember the analogy of the fingers of the hand. Each finger has its own individuality, its own particularity, but each finger is linked to the same hand.

5. Loving yourself sincerely and genuinely is not selfishness. When you achieve such love for yourself, you will notice how this love will overflow abundantly all around you. This is a promise!

6. Death does not exist! You never really die. You have had and will have other lives. Death, as we know it here on Earth, is just a release from one's own creation to begin again other experiences. It is a time of celebration, not pain. The worst thing is not death; it is failing to live your dharma, your dreams.

7. Forgive, forgive, and forgive again, both yourself and those around you. Forgiveness is cleansing and healing. Finally, remember that there is nothing to forgive. You have chosen the script you are living, and the people around you only help you fulfill it.

8. Leave judgment aside. You are judgmental when you consider that "your truth" is different from "the truth of others." Except that there is no absolute truth. Remember the analogy of the points in the sphere. It doesn't matter in how many ways a point is experienced. Eventually they will all converge to the centre of the sphere, represented by God or Source.

9. Be open to life. Don't resist it. Don't obsessively control every detail. Everything happens for a reason. Right now, you are exactly where you need to be!

10. You can learn anything from anyone or anything. Remember the chewing gum!

Those would be the most important lessons. You see, ultimately, perhaps the most important lesson is to allow ourselves to feel. Sometimes the lessons seem easy, and the mind easily intellectualizes them, but they are worth absorbing, worth feeling by the soul and every cell in the body. Remember that when you are open, you see truth and beauty everywhere. Remember that God is silence, and all background noise is just a cheap copy. Remember that we are spirit, soul, and consciousness. Be open to heal, not repress. Finally, be careful not to wear spiritualism as a badge to decorate your ego. Very many people do this. You will notice those who do. There is nothing spiritual about it.

WOMAN: I wrote them all down. I will consider the wisdom of these words.

MONK: So, how do you feel now, after all this talk about your experience with those things that you felt you had, but which brought you so much unhappiness?

WOMAN: I feel much better now that I've found out what that "*something*" means. It's as if my state of wholeness, of fulfillment, is complete. I feel a love that is warm, real, detached, and so universal. I feel blessed, but not overwhelmed or attached. I feel that loving detachment. Thank you for taking the time to remind me of knowing my eternal soul! I am so grateful for everything around me, for the infinity of potential, for the inner joy that simply exists for no particular reason, just realizing that this is the nature of the soul, of being love, joy, and that we have come to this relative plane to experience these aspects of our being. Perhaps, we should listen more to our inner voice and not because we "have to" but because it is worth it. In the end, all we need is within ourselves. We don't live on Earth. We are the Earth.

MONK: I am glad to hear these things! You can go back home and share the wisdom of these words. Now you truly understand the wisdom that *God is a Potato*!

References

1. *Becoming Supernatural* — Dr. Joe Dispenza (or, I like to call it "The New Age Bible." A truly revealing book that outlines spirituality demonstrated by science)

2. *Conversations with God: An Uncommon Dialogue* (Books 1-4) — Neale Donald Walsch

3. *The Complete Dictionary of Ailments and Diseases* — Jacques Martel

4. *The Emotion Code: How to Release Your Trapped Emotions for Abundant Health, Love, and Happiness* — Dr. Bradley B. Nelson

5. *The Body Remembers. The Psychophysiology of Trauma and Trauma Treatment* — Babette Rothschild

6. *Medical Medium: Secrets Behind Chronic and Mystery Illness and How to Finally Heal* — Anthony William

7. *The Power of Your Subconscious Mind. Unlock Your Master Key to Success* — Joseph Murphy

8. *Many Lives, Many Masters* — Dr. Brian Weiss

9. *The Power of Now: A Guide to Spiritual Enlightenment* — Eckhart Tolle

10. *Courageous Souls* — Robert Schwartz

11. *Human by Design: From Evolution by Chance to Transformation by Choice* — Gregg Braden

12. *The Child in You* — Stefanie Stahl

13. *The Divine Matrix. Bridging Time, Space, Miracles, and Belief* — Gregg Braden

Acknowledgments

I will not mention names. Those would just be labels, and science and spirituality have shown us that we are more than that. We are more than any ideology, name, age, nationality, or any other label. You are more than your name, I am more than my name, we are more than our names. So, all thanks and gratitude goes to the Divine Source, the Infinite Intelligence, to every co-creative soul experiencing the beauty of this life.

To Everything and Nothing, infinite gratitude.

Namaste!

www.ingramcontent.com/pod-product-compliance
Lightning Source LLC
Chambersburg PA
CBHW031339060726
47590CB00007B/2540